D1122013

RIVERSIDE CITY COLLEGE

LIBRARY

Riverside, California

Getting Together

A Guide to
Sexual Enrichment for Couples

Getting Together

A Guide to
Sexual Enrichment for Couples

Drs. Leon and Shirley Zussman
WITH JEREMY BRECHER

William Morrow and Company, Inc.
New York 1979

Library of Congress Cataloging in Publication Data

Zussman, Leon.
    Getting together.

        Bibliography: p.
        Includes index.
        1. Sex in marriage.   2. Sex instruction.
I. Zussman, Shirley, joint author.   II. Brecher,
Jeremy, joint author.   III. Title.
HQ31.Z83   1979   301.41'8   78-13431
ISBN 0-688-03383-0

Printed in the United States of America.

First Edition

1   2   3   4   5   6   7   8   9   10

To Virginia E. Johnson and William H. Masters, M.D., whose enormous contribution to the knowledge of human sexual response and the treatment of sexual inadequacy has enriched many lives, including the lives of those who have tried to follow in their footsteps. Many of the exercises described in this book are adapted from their pioneering work in the field of sex therapy.

Contents

Getting Together

A Guide to
Sexual Enrichment for Couples

One

Raising Your Sexual IQ

This is a book for couples in love who want to enrich and enhance their lives together by strengthening the physical and emotional bond between them. For most people a close sexual relationship is a source of great pleasure which ripples over into the rest of their life. When there is dissatisfaction and frustration in the sexual part of a couple's relationship, sex often serves as a wedge to separate them.

Today new information and a more permissive social climate are making it possible for couples to derive greater pleasure from physical intimacy. Even the pain and distress of a sexual problem may be treated successfully as the result of the monumental contribution of Dr. William Masters and Virginia Johnson. Their book *Human Sexual Inadequacy* has brought new hope to the lives of many people.

Getting Together focuses on enhancing the quality of communication and sexuality between men and women. It is not aimed at those experiencing serious sexual dysfunction, but rather is directed toward readers eager to achieve a more fulfilling sex life. To do this, we think it is necessary to dispel myths and misconceptions that have been our cultural heritage from the past and have interfered with optimum sexual pleasure. We also encourage exploration of individual attitudes in an attempt to increase each reader's knowledge of his or her own sexuality.

We view sexuality as a broad spectrum of experiences from which people draw in accordance with their particular needs and desires and within their particular value system. These needs and desires may vary from one occasion to another, from one stage of life to another, and may be interwoven with innumerable factors in one's life situation, such as health and illness, joy and sorrow, and the capacity for inti-macy and closeness.

We believe that people express their sexuality not only through a physical relationship but through the way in which they identify themselves as human beings and relate to the people around them. There are no standards to meet, no goals that must be reached, no rules except a responsibility not to hurt others or allow yourself to be hurt. To the extent that you can give pleasure, you get pleasure in return. If you want to get really close to another person, sharing your sexuality is the most intense form of communication available.

CAN THIS BOOK HELP YOU?

One way to find out if you can profit from this book is to test your sexual IQ:

- Do you define sex as intercourse?
- Do you believe sex should be spontaneous?
- Do you feel it is selfish to concentrate on your own responses?
- Do you think that you can will an erection or an orgasm?

- Do you think it is the man's responsibility to see to it that his partner reaches a climax?
- Do you think that if a man is able to control his ejaculation long enough most women will have an orgasm?
- Do you think that having an orgasm during intercourse is the "normal" way for women to experience orgasm?
- Do you strive for simultaneous orgasm with your partner?
- Do you feel that if a man fails to get an erection from time to time it is a sign that he's over the hill?
- Do you think that people lose their interest in sex as they get older?
- Are you unable to express to your partner your wishes, needs, and desires?

If your answer to most of these questions is in the affirmative, we feel that this book can be of considerable value in correcting the myths and misconceptions that you, like most people in our society, still adhere to.

The book is written in a style that we feel meets a need on the part of many people for accurate information presented in a framework that views sex as an integral part of one's total life. During the two years that we were special correspondents on the NBC National Radio News and Information Service, broadcasting daily on Human Relations and Human Sexuality, we were frequently asked to recommend reading material that would supplement our broadcasts. Included among our recommendations were many excellent books written primarily for professionals by authorities in the field of sex therapy. For most of our audience these books required an academic and scientific background they did not have, although they gleaned useful information from them.

Popular books on either male or female sexuality were also recommended. However, there were few books that focused on couples, that could be easily read and understood, without the distraction of pictures or drawings that provided models of youth and beauty that are difficult for most people to identify with.

Who We Are and What We Do

We are currently engaged in private practice for the treatment of sexual dysfunction and the promotion of sexual enrichment. One of us is a gynecologist-obstetrician; the other is a psychotherapist. Over the last eight years more than eight hundred couples, ranging in age from nineteen to seventy-five, in many walks of life, have come to us with a wide range of sexual difficulties. Our treatment plan is modeled on the principles of Masters and Johnson, with some modifications.

Sexual Enrichment

We have also seen many couples who would like to achieve greater intimacy but do not require sex therapy, because they do not have the kind of serious sexual dysfunction for which the Masters-Johnson methods were originally designed. Others may not want to spend the time or money. And some couples don't consider it appropriate to their personal life-styles. Over the past few years we have also conducted sexual enrichment seminars throughout the country. These seminars are designed for people who are eager to increase their knowledge of their own sexuality and that of their partners.

Who attends these seminars? Let us tell you about one such couple, Lucy and Will. They were attractive, intelligent people in their late thirties and had been married for eight years. Lucy put her reasons for coming this way.

I really started thinking about our sex life when I got the feeling that somehow the sexual revolution was passing us by. What's going on makes you look at yourself more, and wonder whether you're enjoying sex as much as you could. I don't mean having sex with lots of partners or trying everything you might see in a porno movie, but I'd really like to catch up with the sexual revolution in the sense of feeling freer to talk with Will about sex, and overcoming some of the hang-ups I still seem to have about it. Then there are some more specific things, too; for example, I'd really like it if Will could be more aggressive sometimes, but I don't know how to ask him without hurting his feelings. If we could deal with some of these things, I have a sense that things would go better in other spheres as well.

Will similarly described his reasons for attending:

Our sex life used to be something really important to us, but lately it seems as if it is getting to be almost a chore, something you do because it is expected, but not something you really look forward to with anticipation. It seems hard to get away from the pattern we've established—usually just on weekends, and always in pretty much the same way. It's comfortable and I still enjoy it, but it doesn't seem to be going anywhere. The other parts of our lives are moving along, developing in ways we like—work, friends, family, our hobbies. And I have the feeling that if only we knew how to go about it, that could begin to happen with our sexual relationship too.

OUR PHILOSOPHY OF SEXUALITY

Our interest in sexual enrichment is a reflection of our philosophy of sexuality: we see sexuality as a dimension of personality, a way of being and relating, which is an integral part of our total existence. In every aspect of our lives we are sexual people, because sexuality cannot be separated from the total mosaic of our human nature. The physical aspect of our sexuality is a normal, natural function which, unlike other physiological functions such as digestion or breathing, is enormously influenced by the society we live in, the family that reared us, and the interaction with our partner.

In addition, we do not equate sex with intercourse. Rather, we view sex as a broad panorama of experiences— touching, kissing, holding, looking, tasting, smelling—all of which are pleasurable in their own right. Thinking of sex as play, with no goal in view, removes it from the pressured world outside the bedroom. To reduce the pressures within the bedroom, we recommend that couples start touching and caressing and enjoying contact, wherever it may take them. As one of our patients described it, "Before I came for therapy, I wanted to reach Paris, but we're having so much fun sightseeing along the way, it no longer seems important whether we get there or not." Eventually she did achieve orgasms as she had hoped, but the important discovery for her and her husband was that overemphasis on the end result reduces both the possibility of achieving that result and the pleasure of the total experience.

A crucial part of our philosophy is our belief that a good sex life depends not so much upon the skill or prowess of an individual as upon the quality of the human relationship within which sex takes place. While some individuals can enjoy a casual sexual encounter, most people seem to prefer sex with a lover to whom they are emotionally committed.

A true sexual partnership can be one of the most fulfilling

of all experiences. It involves a giving and taking, a mutuality of intimacy and satisfaction, rarely available in other relationships. And it requires an implicit trust, an ease of communication, and a freedom of self-expression that are among the most valued qualities of human life. The purpose of this book, then, is to help you and your loved one become true sexual partners in this far-reaching sense.

This approach to sex as something in which both partners are involved is also one of the central features of contemporary sex therapy. Where possible we don't treat one or the other partner separately; we treat the couple. When only one member of a couple comes to us, we encourage him or her to bring the other partner into the therapy process. We find that difficulties which may seem insurmountable when dealt with individually can usually be overcome when both partners participate.

For the same reasons we have designed this book to be used by a couple. Creating a better love life isn't up to one or the other of you; it is a cooperative enterprise. You can use this book as an aid in that joint venture. Even if you do not have a regular sexual partner at present, you may gain some new insights and information from reading this book that will enhance your future relationships.

Sharing this book with your mate is one way you can start things moving toward a better sexual partnership. If you've looked it over or read it yourself and feel it might be helpful, suggest that your loved one take a look at it. Consider reading it together as an opportunity to open up discussion about your love life. Many times both partners secretly wish they could discuss intimate matters, but neither one knows how to break the ice. This is a chance for both of you to get things you've been thinking and feeling out in the open. Sharing this book can be a way of communicating your desire to make your partnership fuller, richer, and more loving.

The Design of Our Program

Much of our sexual enrichment program consists of sexual *reeducation*. We find that this reeducation can itself play a major role in reducing the anxieties and inappropriate expectations which often disrupt sexual pleasure and functioning. We hope that by reading this book you will be able to acquire some of the reeducation you would receive if you came to us for therapy or attended our sexual enrichment seminars.

Learning by Doing

Obviously, you can't expect to transform your sex life simply by reading this or any other volume. The way to change is to try out the new information you have been given, experiment with it, and see how it works out in your own bedroom.

This active, practical approach is another of the keys to modern sex therapy. We don't just talk with our patients; we give them "homework assignments," sexual experiences to try out in the privacy of their own bedrooms. Many couples find these the most effective part of our program.

In this book we have also included many exercises for you to try out. Each one is designed to be an enjoyable experience in mutual exploration and communication, whether verbal or nonverbal. All have proven useful for a significant proportion of the couples we have seen over the years. The value of some may not be evident to you at first, but we urge you to try them anyway—you are likely to enjoy them!

Take your time, and see how much pleasure and understanding you can get from each.

Set aside at least an hour or two when neither of you is too tired or pressured to try these exercises. In today's hurried world, this may not always be so easy. But for busy couples especially, setting aside a relaxed occasion for mutual pleasure may in itself be the best starting point for enhancing your love life.

Every couple will react to the suggestions in their own unique way. We have described some of these reactions below in order to illustrate some of the possibilities these exercises can open up, as well as some of the difficulties that may be met along the way.

How to Use This Book

This book can be used in a number of different ways, depending on your own needs and feelings. Talk it over and see which one is right for you:

• You may just want to read it through and discuss it with your partner. For many couples this can be very useful. It can give you a common body of facts and approaches that you can try out on your own. And it can help you initiate new lines of communication.

• You may want to use the book as a study guide for your own do-it-yourself sexual enrichment program. Many couples can benefit most from going through the book chapter by chapter, discussing how each section applies to them, and trying all the suggestions in the order in which they appear. You may want to arrange to set aside an hour or two for this purpose at least twice a week for a month or two.

• Or you may want to use the book in a less structured way, picking it up when you feel in the mood and trying out various ideas and suggestions that appeal to you. You can take turns picking out the things to try. (If one of you seems to take the initiative consistently, you might discuss why; perhaps it is also the pattern of your sexual relationship. You can use this as an opportunity to discuss that pattern.

Regardless of the way the two of you choose to use this book, in all probability it will add new dimensions to your sexuality. You should not make it a goal-oriented task; that will only add pressure and tension to your efforts. Remember, getting there is half the fun!

COMMON CONCERNS ABOUT SEX THERAPY

There are certain questions most people ask about any program designed to improve their sex lives. These same questions come up repeatedly following our lectures, and during our sexual enrichment seminars and therapy sessions. No doubt they have occurred to you as well. They usually grow out of misconceptions people have about sex therapy, based on what they have heard or read.

It's Not Mechanical

Perhaps the most common misconception about sex therapy is that it is based on mechanistic or even acrobatic exercises. One woman told us: "From what I've heard, it all sounds terribly mechanical, like a set of exercises that makes sex something like operating a machine, not something warm and loving and human. Maybe it would work that way for some people, but for me I feel that both the problems and the pleasures of sex are too involved with my feelings for mechanical exercises to do me any good."

She was quite surprised when we said that we agreed with her completely. Mechanical exercises, we explained, would be more likely to make a sexual relationship worse, not just for her but for most people. Both sexual problems and sexual satisfactions do indeed have their roots in the realm of feeling. As mentioned earlier, we do suggest various homework assignments for partners to try, but they are not mechanical exercises; rather, they are experiences which can help couples to learn new ways of feeling and relating. No matter how precisely the directions were followed, most of these exercises would be pointless unless they allowed the partners to explore and express their own moods, emotions, inclinations, and desires. Above all, they are designed to enhance communication between partners, and thereby enable them to experience and express their sexual feelings more fully.

Enjoy, Don't Perform

A second common concern is that a program for sexual improvement will make demands for performance that will leave people feeling threatened and inadequate. A man put it this way:

> I already feel under pressure every time we start the sexual preliminaries. I worry: will I stay firm? Will I ejaculate too soon? Will I be able to satisfy her? The last thing I need is to be given further tests to pass or fail. If that's what you do in this program, I'm just not up to it. More pressure to perform would just make me feel tenser and more likely to fail.

He was right. Pressure to perform is the way to make sex worse, not better. As we told him:

> Far from demanding performance, our aim is to help you learn that in the pleasure world of sex you can forget all about the need to perform and for a time dedicate your-

selves to mutual and intense pleasure. At no time is either partner instructed to achieve anything in the way of sexual performance. Instead, our techniques are designed to help *eliminate* the pressure to perform, which itself is one of the main causes of sexual difficulty.

You Are Not to Blame

Another anxiety is common when couples consider try-ing to improve their sex lives: which one of them will be held responsible for the fact that there are problems? We remember one couple who expressed this concern. When we met with them separately, the male partner confided:

> A lot of the time I believe it's all my fault, and that makes me feel just awful. But at other times, she just seems so angry and demanding that I feel she's really the one to blame.

His mate said:

> There are a lot of things in the way he acts toward me sexually that just make me resent him terribly; I'm afraid that if I let that anger out it will hurt him, maybe even drive him away. But I'm also afraid that maybe he'll be able to twist this whole thing around so that it will seem as if I'm responsible for all our troubles. And sometimes I even think maybe I am.

This couple was not unusual. Often couples are filled with both guilt about their own role and anger at their partner's behavior. They fear that sex therapy may intensify these feelings. As we explained to one couple:

> When a chemist tries to explain why vinegar and baking soda bubble wildly when they are mixed, he doesn't look only at the properties of one or the other substance. Instead,

he looks at the interaction between the two of them. It's the same with sex therapy: we don't focus on what's wrong with one or the other partner, but on the interaction between them. We view any sexual difficulty as belonging to the couple as such. And we look at solving it as a cooperative project for both, not as a task for either one alone.

As a matter of fact, in most cases when a couple has sexual difficulties, both partners usually contribute. Sexual difficulties are a shared problem because they arise from a shared activity. It follows, then, that improving things should be a shared endeavor.

Two

Making Time for Intimacy

It is often pointed out that our society is preoccupied with sex. Advertisements appealing to the viewer's sexual interest flood TV. Sex is a frequent theme in books, movies, magazines, and other media. We are bombarded with sexually provocative material designed to exploit our natural interest in sex for commercial purposes.

Yet, despite the emphasis on sex, your daily life is likely to be quite inhospitable to sexual pleasure. Most people have to follow carefully planned schedules, working at jobs and taking care of homes and children. Often they are under considerable pressure to perform at work or at home, which results in feelings of tension and stress. You have to discipline yourself to do what you have to do, not what would give you enjoyment and pleasure at the moment. You spend most of your day among people whom you relate to impersonally, rarely reaching out to touch them. Most of the time, a spontaneous expression of any kind, particularly of a physical nature, no matter how casual, would be considered inappropriate or even shocking.

It is hard to keep the restraints imposed by society from affecting your emotional life with your partner. You may find yourself tense and fatigued at the end of the day. Similarly, you may find that your tendency during the day to control the spontaneous expression of your feelings carries over to the evening. The result can be to eliminate from your life the relaxed free time that is necessary for you to reveal and express sexual responsiveness.

As one highly successful executive put it, "I never have any unstructured time. I'm always doing something I'm supposed to do. Even when I come home, things are structured—having a drink before dinner, the dinner hour, time with the children—as well as all kinds of social engagements. Most of it I enjoy, but the idea of some time with no 'shoulds' attached to it, sounds like the most luxurious thing I can think of."

This situation is aggravated by the low priority many people give to sex in their daily lives. People have time for work, movies, TV, chores, dinner parties, cleaning the house, mowing the lawn—but often find they are too busy or too tired to make love. How many couples would turn down an invitation to go out to dinner, to play cards, or to see a movie in order to spend a few private hours together— touching, holding, sharing, exploring each other, tuning in to their partner's responses and their own sensual feelings? And how many choose, instead, to fill their leisure hours with other activities until they are too exhausted to give sex the energy and attention it deserves?

Sexual activity between partners is not always honored as an activity that is planned for, for which time is set aside, or which even takes place at optimum times, when both partners are relaxed and rested. Instead, it seems, for many, to be relegated to a time when there is nothing left to do.

MAKING A DATE

We believe that in our busy world, it is essential for couples to plan special times to be together for the sole purpose of enjoying each other. We suggest actually making a date, as you would to go out to dinner or play tennis or golf. This date could be a chance for you to spend private, uninterrupted time together, enjoying each other's company, without any demands or expectations of what you will do, where you will go, how you will feel. It gives you an opportunity to leave the tensions of the day behind, and let your feelings and sensations take over.

You can make a date anywhere from half an hour to a day or more in advance. Take turns asking; one can simply say, "How about a date tonight after dinner?" * If occasionally you find yourselves together with free time and in the mood, there is of course no reason you shouldn't go ahead without a prior engagement.

Some people have reservations about this idea at first. As one woman put it, "I feel that sex should be spontaneous, something you do when you are in the mood. It seems unnatural to make it something you plan for."

We agree that sex should be spontaneous. But we live in a society which thwarts our spontaneity. Therefore we have to create opportunities when we *can* spontaneously express our feelings and our sexuality. (Similarly, a painter may depend upon spontaneous inspiration, but he has to plan time to spend with his paints and easel if he is to make use of it.) Planning occasions together doesn't mean deciding in advance to have intercourse; what you actually do with this

---

* Or you might try telephoning from the office during the day to set up an appointment before dinner.

time should depend completely on what you and your mate feel like doing at the moment. But it does mean a mutual agreement to exclude other preoccupations and enjoy each other.

Underlying the resistance to planning time for sex is often a lingering belief, acquired in childhood, that it is wrong to desire sex, that sexual feelings are not something to be honored. For example, if a woman feels that she is the recipient or victim of sex, if sex is just something that she accepts passively, she may also feel that she is not responsible for it. Planning times for sexual activity requires that you recognize and honor your own interest in sex and take responsibility for fulfilling it. This may be somewhat threatening, especially for unmarried partners who may feel somewhat guilty about their relationship. But it also creates an opportunity for you to show your partner that you genuinely want to be with him or her, to give and receive pleasure.

Making time for dates may take careful planning, particularly if both of you work at different hours, or if one of you spends considerable time traveling. An overscheduled social life, responsibility for young children, or a pattern of spending free time with relatives and friends can similarly interfere. Sit down together, examine your schedules, and figure out how you can make time to be alone together. Many responsibilities can't be avoided, but every couple can find ways to be together intimately several times a week—unless they are using their other activities as excuses to avoid intimacy.

Making the date is the first step in creating a situation where you can in fact leave behind the pressures and patterns of the demanding, pleasure-denying world. In contrast to a sudden decision to hop into bed, making a date in advance allows time for transition to an erotic mood.

It allows you to anticipate the pleasures to come, to let loving feelings and expectations roll around a bit in the back of your mind, to fantasize the situation ahead. As one woman put it, "When we make a date in the morning, it makes me feel slightly but pleasantly aroused all day. By the time it arrives, I often feel much more eager for sex than I would otherwise."

Of course, you won't always feel in the mood for sex when the time for the date arrives, but often, if you just relax together, talk and caress each other, your mood may change. Therefore, it is a good idea to set aside time for dates on a regular basis. Otherwise you may find that days, weeks, or sometimes even months pass without the time for physical intimacy. For the same reasons, if your partner asks you for a date, don't turn it down unless you are ill or really out of sorts, or faced with an unexpected obligation that cannot be postponed. Rather, just begin and see how things go. It's been our experience that getting into the mood doesn't really begin until you start stroking, caressing, holding each other, probably because everyone needs to be reminded that those things feel good.

If one of you is a day person and the other a night person, talk to your partner about it and try varying the time you make love. Take turns initiating lovemaking, choose the time that is best for you. Ask your partner to go along with you—and express your willingness to cooperate when he or she initiates lovemaking.

"THE GREATEST THING WE LEARNED"

Karen and Martin were one of those couples who make the rest of us wonder, "Where do they get the time and the energy?" In addition to his busy law practice, Martin was active in half a dozen public-interest groups and committees; many of his weekends were spent running camping trips for the Boy Scouts. Karen, besides taking care of their three children, held a full-time teaching job and handled the accounts for their church.

At one of our early sessions with them, we suggested a specific exercise for them to try at home during the following week. When they came to their next session, they reported that they hadn't tried it until the night before for the simple reason that they had not had a single evening all week when both were home, awake, and not exhausted.

We discussed together whether they really wanted to put physical intimacy high on their priority list, and if so, how this could reasonably be worked out. People's sexual interest varies from time to time due to many interwoven physical and emotional factors. We pointed out that they didn't have to feel there had to be a standard they had to meet. Needs and priorities vary, but what is important is for both partners to share their feelings about this, to avoid resentment and misunderstanding. Karen and Martin agreed that they wanted and needed more closeness and intimacy than they had experienced recently. They had allowed all their outside activities to intervene. Somehow the idea of planning had never occurred to them.

We told them:

Look, you plan everything else in your life. You plan your ski weekends, even though you don't know whether or not it's going to snow. You schedule going to church services on Sunday, although you have no idea whether you will be open to religious inspiration on any given Sunday or not. As for getting in the mood, the key usually lies in arousing your expectations. The best way to put yourself in the mood is to make a date so that both of you have "equal time" to fantasize in advance.

Martin said:

I see your point. Sometimes I come home from work and I've been daydreaming about sex all afternoon. But Karen is busy feeding the kids and obviously not in the mood for it. Often I have to go to meetings in the evening—maybe she's longing for sex while I'm gone, but by the time I get home she's usually asleep. I think we should give this dating idea a try.

Karen said with a smile:

Something in me keeps saying, "A good girl wouldn't think of planning for a thing like that," but I guess that's silly. Why don't we take next Saturday, send the kids to my mother's, and see if we can't just enjoy ourselves for the day?

We suggested that they think of something to do—in addition to making love—that they would particularly enjoy. Martin said, "Before we were married we loved to look at prints and paintings, but we just haven't seemed to have the time to do it for years. Why don't I stop by the library and pick up some art books? It seems there's a whole part of ourselves we've lost touch with, that maybe we can recapture."

At our next session they told us that Saturday had been one of the memorable days of their lives. They had sent the kids off to Karen's mother's Friday night. Saturday morning they slept late, made themselves breakfast and ate it in bed, and spent most of the morning just touching and holding and caressing. By that time they were relaxed enough for a little fantasy. One of their fondest memories was of a boat cruise they had taken on their first anniversary, and they decided to imagine that they were back in their old stateroom. Karen even unearthed the nightgown she had worn on the cruise, and together they recaptured the mood of the trip. Free from the pressures of their busy life, they found their feelings of pleasure and warmth were greatly enhanced. Afterward they took a shower together and celebrated with a bottle of champagne, which Karen had hidden away in the back of the refrigerator. The rest of the afternoon they spent poring over art books and fantasizing planning trips to world-famous museums.

By the time the children came home that evening, Karen and Martin were feeling closer and more relaxed than they had felt for ages. They realized that they had to make time in their lives for each other. In fact, several months later, at the end of the program, Martin told us, "The greatest thing we learned was this concept of the date. Days and even weeks used to roll by while we waited for an occasion when we both were free and in the mood. Making a date lets us find the time, and gives us a chance to get ourselves in the mood. We've given being together—not just sex—a higher priority in our lives."

PROTECTING YOUR PRIVACY

Once you have set aside time to spend together exploring mutual pleasure, the next thing is to ensure your privacy. For many couples, the biggest problem is children. "I'm always nervous that the kids will overhear, or come barging in," one person told us, and such concerns are common.

We believe that everyone is entitled to privacy. All members of a family, both parents and children, should be able to go into their own rooms and feel safe from intrusion. Children should be taught that both they and their parents have this right, which all family members should respect. If you respect your children's privacy, by example they will learn to respect yours. Lock your bedroom door; if you don't have a lock, buy one. Consider this privacy something to use not only for intercourse, but simply for reading the paper, lying naked on the bed, talking, masturbating, or anything else you feel like doing in private.

There is no reason children (or other relatives) should know the details of your sexual life. But the knowledge that their parents enjoy each other emotionally and physically and have a private life together is the best preparation children can have for their own sexual development.

Children make many demands on parents' time, of course, even when the right to privacy is respected. Sometimes it is a pleasant relief to make a date for a time when the children are away visiting relatives, staying over with friends, at school, or when you can make other arrangements to care for them. Take advantage of such opportunities, but don't wait for them to make dates for mutual pleasure.

Another invader of privacy is the telephone. Somehow it always seems to ring just when you are getting ready to make love. Fortunately, it is easy to silence: just take the receiver off the hook. This indicates that you are busy —as indeed you are. If for some reason you have to know who is calling you, you may want to purchase a machine that records phone messages, but in most cases taking the phone off the hook should be sufficient.

Any other likely intrusions can be dealt with just as directly. If you live in a community where neighbors drop in on each other unannounced, put a note on your door saying "Busy till 5:30." If your in-laws habitually come by, ask them to phone first. Remember, you have a right to privacy.

YOUR SEXUAL ENVIRONMENT

Next, create an appropriate milieu. Here the most important step is for each of you to explore your own reactions, negative and positive, to the physical setting of your sexual activity. If you like pillows, buy some extra ones. Small pillows to tuck in here and there are very useful to make various positions more comfortable. Are you tired of the curtains in your bedroom? Put up some new ones. Invest in a large comfortable bed; after all, you spend a third of your life in it. Is your bedroom too cold in winter to be naked in comfort? Get a space heater and warm the room up beforehand. If the lights are glaring get a softer light or a dimming device; or put a light in the closet or outside the door. You are responsible for making yourself comfortable and creating a sensuous environment. Don't be afraid to pamper yourself.

Your mate is of course the most important part of your erotic environment. There may be certain things you would like your partner to do to enhance the sexual atmosphere, but you are afraid to mention them for fear of exposing yourself or offending him or her. Expressing your feelings without criticizing your partner is essential. To say, "You smell, why don't you ever take a shower before we make love," is an attack. To say, "I enjoy being close to you when you're clean and fresh," is a straightforward and uncritical statement of your own feelings. If you like a particular type of perfume, tell your partner, "I feel turned on when you use that scent."

GETTING STARTED

As time for your date approaches, you should try to relax in the way that works best for you. Many people find that a cocktail or a glass of wine does the trick. (Remember, though, that more than one drink is likely to make you drowsy, and that too much alcohol depresses sexual response.) Try a warm bath or shower, listen to music, take a short nap. If you like, do relaxation or yoga exercises or even have a wrestling match with your partner. Try anything that signals to your nerves, muscles, and brain that the pressures and demands of the day are over, that they can cease performing and instead help you to relax and enjoy yourself.

Your first task is to create a proper context for sex, one that is lacking when you watch TV all evening and then simply get into bed and expect to have intercourse. Some kinds of conversation are usually inappropriate. If you've been pleased or upset by something that happened during the day, you can talk about how you feel—but don't dwell on it. This is a chance to leave the preoccupations of work and family responsibilities behind. Similarly this is not the time for intellectual discussion—even about sex. Such exchanges of ideas are best accomplished when you are alone together at the dinner table, or taking a walk or a drive. Don't get so wrapped up in ideas that you fail to experience your sensations and feelings. Use conversation to express your feelings of love, affection, tenderness, concern, and support. Let such verbal communication and the nonverbal communication of touching and holding mutually reinforce each other.

Consider your dates a chance to engage in spontaneous play. Humans, like other mammals, seem to have a need for

physical and interpersonal play. Watch two little puppies
or toddlers playing; it is all fun and games, enjoying their
bodies, rolling around, smelling and feeling each other, and
creating a world of imagination. They feel good; they feel
hard or soft or smooth; and they enjoy it. It's a pleasure
just to watch them. Yet such play is hardly considered
respectable for adults in our society, unless it takes the form
of a highly competitive sport or game with rigid rules and
an emphasis on performance. See if you can recapture some
of the playful spirit of childhood, in which you can imagine
and act out whatever you feel like, pursue whatever catches
your fancy, and do things for no purpose except the pleasure of doing them.

When you make a date don't feel that it always has to end
in intercourse. Intercourse can be an intensely pleasurable
experience and certainly should be fully enjoyed when that
is what you both want. But too often lovemaking is viewed
as a hierarchy, with intercourse at the top and other activities of lesser importance. We view lovemaking on a con-
tinuum with no one activity given greater importance than
another. The important element is the pleasure derived,
whatever the particular activity. Be prepared for intercourse
when you get together in case intercourse does occur, so you
don't have to interrupt lovemaking to put in your dia-
phragm, for example, but don't assume it must occur. In
fact, we urge that you occasionally agree beforehand that
you will not have intercourse to ensure an opportunity to
give and get pleasure without any feeling of demand or
pressure to perform.

GETTING "TURNED ON"

Sexual arousal is not something that can be willed. It is
an automatic reflex response. But you can deliberately elim-

inate those things that interfere with it, and try to provide those things that stimulate you and your partner. To do so, you need to study your own feelings and responses to discover what's right for you. At the same time, you have to be willing to respond to the needs and feelings your partner expresses.

Discuss what turns you off and on sexually. Feel free to say, for example, "I love it when you wear a sexy nightgown," or "I love to listen to your voice when we make love." You should try to comply with your partner's requests unless they genuinely turn you off—in which case you should say how *you* feel about them, not what's wrong with them. Remember, there is no right or wrong answer to the question of what is sexually exciting. It is entirely a question of personal preference and personal idiosyncrasy. No matter how unusual or even silly it seems, anything that arouses you is all right if it does no harm to anyone. Everyone's tastes and feelings are different—and vary from time to time. Discuss what each of you likes and dislikes as a team cooperating to create as much pleasure as possible for both of you.

Many couples find it exciting to share a fantasy, or to act one out. Others are stimulated by erotic literature, pictures, records, and other materials. We recommend that you try these various aids and see how you react to them—discover which ones excite you, which distract you. Some people find the use of sexually provocative language arousing, others find it distasteful. Explore how each of you feels about it.

If sex becomes too repetitive, think of ways you can vary it. Try making love in front of the fireplace, in the shower, or even on a secluded terrace. Try a change of scene—take a trip, go camping, or exchange houses for a weekend with another couple. We know a couple who occasionally check into a favorite hotel in their own city to make love in an unfamiliar environment.

When a woman described how boring sex had become for her, we asked her to recall past occasions when she had become aroused. She remembered one time when she and her husband had come home from a romantic movie. He had put the lights low and then slowly, tenderly, undressed her. By the time she was naked, she was highly aroused. We suggested that they relive this enjoyable experience. At first the husband's reaction was that he would feel self-conscious because he would be doing something "according to a script." Nevertheless, he reported several weeks later that they had tried to create the mood of the past experience and his wife had become highly excited. We are not suggesting that this simple formula solved the problem of boredom for this couple, but it was the beginning of increasing interest in sexual play for both husband and wife. As the four of us discussed it together, what was really a turning point was that both became aware of the wife's need for a slow prelude to sex and her pleasure that her husband was willing to pay attention to her needs.

Another couple, very elegant people with impeccable manners, had largely lost interest in sex after twenty years of marriage. Each had private sexual desires and fantasies, but each feared to express them lest the other disapprove. The woman told us, "It would turn me on if he would sometimes use gutter language, and call me his whore. But how can I tell him that—what would he think of me?" Her husband said separately, "I would love to put up a mirror in our bedroom so we could watch ourselves making love. I suggested it once, but she thought the idea was really weird."

We explained to each of them that such desires were perfectly normal and that they should go ahead and express them, but that each should be prepared to honor requests from the other. We suggested they go home and discuss frankly just what each would like to hear, see, touch, taste, and smell in conjunction with their lovemaking.

They came back to the next session and reported on the results. They had put up a mirror in their bedroom, much to his satisfaction. But he had drawn the line at the "dirty" words—"I was always taught not to use them, and I just can't bring myself to do it now," he said. We asked her, "How about if you said them yourself—would that do the trick?" She said, "I don't know; I guess I could try it."

Next session they told us that she had tried it, and that it had been very successful. More surprising, it had turned him on too, although he still couldn't bring himself to use the "vulgar" language himself. But some of the rigidity in the way they perceived themselves and each other had begun to dissolve, leaving room for further exploration of their secret desires.

The Role of Fantasy

Only you can know what you find pleasurable and exciting, so you have to take responsibility for creating the conditions you desire. One technique used by both men and women for increasing arousal is fantasy. Many people feel worried or guilty about their sexual fantasies. Often they fear their fantasies are abnormal. A woman told us, "Sometimes I get highly aroused by imagining that I'm being attacked, or that I'm being held down by a group of faceless men. But I try to keep from imagining such things; I think there must be something sick about them."

A man said, "It turns me on to fantasize making love

with a woman and a man at the same time; I've never revealed this to anyone before because it makes me think I must really be a homosexual." In reality, such fantasies —and others far more unusual—are entirely normal. The fact that such thoughts excite you in fantasy doesn't mean that you will act that way in reality. The thought is not the action. Nor do such fantasies necessarily represent desires people want to act out in reality; rather they serve as tools to heighten arousal. Or, at times, fantasies are a way of trying out parts of our personality that we do not want to reveal in real life. For example, a dominating, independent man may enjoy fantasizing himself in a passive role, with a bevy of handmaidens catering to his every whim; a woman may enjoy being aggressive and dominating in her fantasy but feel somewhat hesitant to demonstrate this aspect of herself in the actual lovemaking situation.

You may want to try out in your mind a form of sexual activity that attracts you but that you would hesitate to experiment with in real life. Fantasy can be playful and exciting, but occasionally it can startle or even frighten you. If the latter is so, talking over the content of your fantasy with someone can often be reassuring or help you to understand yourself better.

Many people also worry that their fantasies are somehow disloyal to their partner. This is especially true if they fantasize about someone besides their partners—a personal acquaintance, a movie star, a well-known sex symbol, or even someone they passed on the street. But again, such fantasies usually are thoughts, not acts. They don't usually mean you've lost interest in your partner. Moreover, if a fantasy arouses you it is contributing to your partner's pleasure as well as your own. Of course, if you consistently fantasize making love to another person and only the thought of that person arouses you, the nature of your relationship with your partner needs to be seriously examined.

Exercise: A Time and a Place for Love

Make a date to discuss the questions raised in this chapter at a time when you are both relaxed and in the mood to talk. When the time comes, sit or lie down near each other. Notice if there is anything in your immediate surroundings which makes you feel particularly comfortable or uncomfortable. If you feel sticky, try a shower together. If the light is irritating your eyes, move it or lower it. If you feel thirsty, get something to drink. If your position doesn't feel right, move around till you find one that does. If you fear you may be intruded upon, lock the door. In short, do whatever you can right now to make yourself comfortable and at ease.

Tell your loved one how you feel about the idea of planning time together. Talk over what you like and what you dislike about the idea, whether it makes you feel pressured, whether you might look forward to such times together, how you feel about eliminating other things that are important to you, and the like. Express your feelings about initiating such sessions yourself, and about your partner's initiating them. Make an agreement to try the idea out, to discover whether it works for you.

Don't try to arrange a fixed schedule, but do try to reach agreement on the times and the days that are good for both of you. If your lives are so full of activities that you can't find time, examine your priorities and decide what you can reduce or reschedule.

Talk about ways you can ensure privacy. Take the phone

off the hook for the rest of this discussion. If you don't have a lock on your bedroom door, install one. Share your feelings about privacy in the family. Tell each other about the attitudes toward privacy in the families you grew up in, and how you felt about them. If the right to privacy has not been honored in your family, plan to have a talk about this situation with your children and to make a family rule about respecting each other's privacy.

Tell each other what you like and dislike in your sexual environment, and consider how you can help fulfill each other's needs and desires. Some points to consider include:

SOUND. Many people like music to set the mood; others find it distracting. Are there other noises that distract you? What kind of sounds do you like to hear and make during love play and intercourse? Are you free to make sounds and to accept and enjoy the sounds your partner makes?

TOUCH. What kind of tactile sensations do you like? Would you like to have smoother sheets or softer pillows? What parts of your partner do you like shaved; what parts hairy? Do you like your man to shave before you make love, or do you like the prickly feeling of his beard? If you've gone to bed with night clothes, decide to get into bed together nude from now on.

TASTE. Would you sometimes like a snack, a special cheese or a glass of wine, for instance, before you go to bed? A full meal tends to make people sleepy and dulls sexual appetite and sensation, but a light snack together can be a special treat. If you like the taste of kissing better when your partner has just brushed his or her teeth, say so—you can even make tooth brushing a mutual activity at the start of a date.

SMELL. Everyone has different reactions to smells, which are usually rooted in early childhood experiences. People have little control over the scents they like and dislike—nor do these preferences imply that they necessarily like or dislike the source. Some people like certain perfumes on their partners. Others like the smell of natural body odors. Some prefer to make love only after a shower or bath. We know that many animals are excited sexually by certain chemicals that are emitted by a member of the opposite sex. These chemicals, called pheromones, are produced by women, but we don't yet know their role in sexual arousal. It has not been demonstrated whether men emit these chemicals. We do know, however, that odor does play a role for many men and women in their love play. Tell your partner exactly how you like him or her to smell best—if you like your partner to take a shower, invite him or her to join you in taking one. If you enjoy perfumes and lotions experiment with them.

VISION. Think of what you can do to give your bedroom an erotic ambiance. If the room is too stark, get a curtain, bedspread, or rug for a warmer feeling. If the walls look drab, get some bright posters or whatever else you would like to enliven them. If the room needs a fresh coat of paint, make plans to paint it together. Try candles.

We strongly recommend that a television set not be part of bedroom equipment. Its hypnotic influence tends to separate people rather than permit them to concentrate on each other. It often serves as a means to avoid dealing with a sexual overture and discourages one partner from staying awake if the other is absorbed in a program.

However, the most important part of your visual environment is your partner. Learn to look, to see, to allow your eyes to appreciate the line, the color, the variety of curves in your partner's body. Watch each other dress and undress, and spend as much time as possible in the nude when you are in the privacy of your bedroom.

Now make a date for a specific time within the next several days to spend together for the sole purpose of mutual pleasure. Plan one simple but special thing you would both enjoy—listening to a new record together, reading to each other, sipping some wine, or sharing some special plans.

Imagine you are two single people who have just met. What would you like the other person to know about you? What would you like to know about the other person? The chances are that you will find yourself listening more carefully and responding more enthusiastically to what is being said. Try to carry over some of that same attentiveness to what your partner is saying in your actual relationship. Find the time to really be with each other, to listen, to hear, to convey to each other that this time together is valued.

EXERCISE: WATER PLAY

As part of your date, you might enjoy some water play. When we ask couples if they have ever showered together, many respond that they used to. Although they enjoyed it, the idea got lost in the hustle and bustle of everyday life. If you've never tried it, or if it is a pleasant memory, we suggest that there is no time like the present to get started. Showering together is often the first suggestion we make to the couples who come to us for sex therapy, and almost all report that they enjoyed it a lot. We often recommend that they add it to their permanent repertory of shared pleasures.

There is a sensuous quality to immersing oneself in water, and it often frees one to be playful, to feel fresh and clean and desirable. Take turns inviting each other for a quick, refreshing shower on one occasion, a slow languorous bath on another, or a playful splashing of each other at another time.

This is how we might make the suggestion to you if you were in our office:

"David, invite Lucy to join you in the shower. Pick a time when you're not in a rush to leave the house. Adjust the water to a temperature that's comfortable for both of you. Take turns soaping each other all over. On some occasions exclude the breasts and genitals, on others include them in sexual arousal. This time leave them out so that there's no pressure to perform. When you emerge from the shower, wrap yourselves together in a big towel and pat each other dry. Naked, move to your bed—and we hope you share one bed—or lie down in front of the fireplace if that is possible, still slightly moist and warm. Lie on your sides, with Lucy facing the wall, with David's chest nestling against Lucy's back. Snuggle into her back as closely as you can. We call this the spoon position.

"As you lie together, synchronize your breathing—breathe in and out together. Many people report a feeling of being very close during this experience, a closeness that lingers on long after they've gotten out of bed and begun other activities. This is also a pleasant way to drift off to sleep. On another occasion, try intercourse in this position, with David entering the vagina from the rear. This offers you the opportunity to reach around Lucy with your hands to stimulate her clitoral area; and, Lucy, you can stimulate yourself in this position, with David's hands free to caress other parts of your body. It's a nice position for fantasy."

More Water Play

Another relaxing and sensual experience is to share a bath together. Since bathtubs are not always large enough to accommodate two adults, one can sit in the tub while the other can kneel on some pillows outside the tub and lean over and slowly and gently wash all parts of the bather's body. You can take turns doing this on different nights. Breathing together in the spoon position is a nice way to finish off this experience.

If you're lucky enough to have an outdoor pool which affords privacy, swimming nude together is a very pleasurable form of water play. As in the other exercises in this chapter, the focus should be on the pleasure you derive from it, the expansion of your sensual consciousness. All these experiences need plenty of uninterrupted, private time, earmarked for your partner and yourself.

Three

Getting in Touch

HOW'S YOUR COMMUNICATION?

• *Do you feel that you can express your wishes, needs, and* desires to your loved one without fear of being rejected, ignored, or misunderstood?

• Can you be open and receptive toward your partner, ready to listen with your whole attention to what he or she is trying to convey to you in words or in body language?

• Do you both feel free to ask for the kind of lovemaking you desire, to experiment, to explore new ways of making love?

The first key to good sex is good communication. Sex is, after all, the most intimate form of communication. It is unlikely that a couple who have difficulty in communicating with each other outside of the bedroom will be open and trusting with each other in the privacy of their bedroom. Therefore, when couples come to us with a sexual problem, we spend considerable time in helping them improve their general communication. As partners find it easier to express their feelings to each other, both through talking and through touch, they find that much of the anxiety and tension surrounding sex dissolves and many aspects of their relationship become more pleasurable. This chapter is designed to open up possibilities for communication that you may not have explored.

"HE NEVER TALKS TO ME"

One of the complaints we hear most frequently is the lack of communication between partners. Often, the wife will say her husband never listens to her, and the husband will complain that his wife never talks to him, or vice versa. On the other hand, we also see many couples who think they have good communication, and who, in fact, have no problem exchanging ideas, but who are rarely open about their feelings. Being open is particularly important in sexual matters because there is no other way for your partner to know what you want and need unless you express your feelings.

Unfortunately many people are guarded in their interchange with each other, even though they want to be close and intimate. Let us examine some of the mistakes that block meaningful communication.

"NEVER SAY 'I'"

If you have trouble in general expressing your feelings and your needs to your partner, some of the roots of this difficulty probably go back to your childhood experience. One woman from a strict religious background told us:

> I was taught never to start a sentence with "I"; if I did so I was told I was selfish. It took years before I learned that it was all right to ask for even the smallest thing for myself, and I still have a lot of trouble doing so.

A successful businessman told us:

> When I was growing up, expressing emotions was taboo.
> If I felt angry, I was made to feel there was something bad
> about that. If I felt hurt, I was discouraged from showing
> it. Even the expression of loving feelings was frowned upon.
> Although my parents probably loved us, there was very little
> evidence of that around my house.

Another man reported similar early experiences:

> In my family, any expression of emotion was jumped on
> as a sign of weakness. If my mother cried, my father would
> never comfort her. Instead, he would tell her to control her-
> self and stop acting like a child. When my father would
> come home steamed up over something that had happened
> at work, my mother didn't sympathize; she'd say something
> that implied he probably deserved whatever had happened
> to him.

As a result, he repressed his emotions: instead of getting
angry, he became sullen and withdrawn. If he needed tenderness and support, he couldn't ask for it directly.

"It's Unmanly." "It's Not Feminine."

Our society has laid out strict rules for the ways in which
men and women are supposed to behave. Until recently,
parents were anxious to help their children adapt to these
rules, and most adults were reared in a tradition of rather
strict differentiation between appropriate male and female
behavior. Apart from the inequalities these attitudes created
for women in the areas of educational, vocational, and economic opportunity, this role differentiation had a profound
effect on emotional development. Male children were told to

"act like a man, don't cry, be tough." If they behaved in a tender, nurturing way with their playmates, they were criticized or shamed for acting like a "sissy." It is no wonder that many men find it difficult to express their feelings, or to ask for help or comforting. It is not surprising that many men cover up any feelings that they consider feminine by adopting a supermasculine façade.

Female children, on the other hand, have traditionally been taught to assume passive roles, not to be assertive or to pursue actively what they want. And, by the same token, the sexual needs of the female have been neglected; the needs of the male were the focus of interest and concern. This outlook is changing now, but for many women the attitudes ingrained in childhood and adolescence persist.

These stereotypical sex roles tend to reinforce each other. A man who is worried about his "manliness" may feel threatened by the self-assertion of his partner and may therefore overtly or subtly resist her attempts at self-expression. A woman who feels that she needs a strong man to lean on may react with hostility or contempt to her partner's efforts to relax his supermasculine stance. In short, such stereotypical sex roles can make it difficult for both men and women to reveal their true feelings and desires.

THE WORLD BEYOND THE BEDROOM

Meaningful communication is further impeded in our society by other rules of behavior. Frequently, you have to hide your feelings for practical reasons. You may be angry at your boss, but you are likely to get into trouble if you express that anger. You may be attracted to someone on the street, but you are likely to be considered odd or even dangerous if you try to approach that person. You may sometimes feel so frustrated that you want to run away, or curl up in a corner and hide, but you have to keep up appearances and convince others that you are in control of yourself and your actions. In all these cases, you have to block your outpouring of emotion because it conflicts with other objectives.

Inevitably, the restrictions that are necessary in such contexts contaminate your love life to some degree. For example, a businessman who demands a rigid, unemotional obedience from his employees may expect the same kind of compliance from his mate. A woman who spends all day managing a complex household or working in a busy office may consider her partner's feelings simply one more problem to be coped with. Whether or not such attitudes are necessary in society at large, they certainly are inappropriate in an intimate sexual relationship, where they are bound to generate tension and resentment.

"I'm Not O.K."

Often people feel that there is something wrong with them because they harbor feelings they think are wrong. Pearl felt that the jealousy and anger she experienced were an ugly part of her that she did not want to reveal to anyone. Tim, who presented himself as the man in charge, was ashamed because at times he longed to be taken care of. Both Pearl and Tim regarded these feelings as parts of themselves that needed to be hidden from view. Actually, all human beings experience a wide range of emotions, and their appropriate expression is natural and normal.

The fear of revealing your inner feelings can be reduced if you realize that such concerns are universal, that other people —including your partner—experience anger, resentment, envy, etc., just as you do. A mutual recognition and acceptance of these feelings is one of the finest gifts partners in a relationship can give each other.

"You're Not O.K."

It's hard to express your feelings if you fear your partner will reject them. This expectation is often characteristic of people whose emotions were regularly ignored when they were growing up. Admittedly, such exposure does involve a genuine risk of rejection. But everything we do in life involves some risk; the only alternative to taking risks is not to live at all. If you hide your deepest emotions out of fear of rejection, then there is no chance that they will ever be accepted. If your partner does in fact tend to be unresponsive to your intimate disclosures, the solution is not to hide behind a protective barrier but to try to change the relationship so that it is based on a greater feeling of trust which will enable you to be more open and vulnerable with each other.

"Home Again"

What does the ability to communicate have to do with sex? Let us tell you the story of one couple who experienced a serious deterioration of their sex life as a direct result of losing their ability to communicate—and whose relationship improved dramatically when they learned to say and show what they felt.

Jack and Anne were in their mid-forties and had been married for nineteen years. When they came to us, they were having virtually no sexual contact. Over the preceding year, Jack had grown tense and irritable. He flared up easily, and had largely stopped making overtures to Anne. She felt hurt and rejected but couldn't bring herself to say so, out of fear that he would respond negatively to any appeal for tenderness. Instead of telling him how hurt she felt, how great her need for him was, she reacted by nagging and criticizing him for being indifferent in every way to her and the children.

One day, when Jack talked privately with the male therapist, he revealed that he was under great pressure at the office. He was afraid he would lose his job because he had less training in modern business methods than some of the younger men who had recently joined the firm. Jack had not discussed his fears with Anne; he was afraid that she would become panicky. Besides, it was difficult for him to expose what he took to be a sign of inadequacy, let alone reveal the occasional moments of real terror that he had about his future. Anne's criticisms had only reinforced his sense of inadequacy, strengthening his tendency to withdraw from her.

When, in the course of our subsequent joint sessions, Jack was able to tell her how pressured he felt at work, how frightened and insecure he was, and how it led him to act the way he did, he was quite surprised at her reaction. He had felt sure she would be resentful and even contemptuous of him; but far from being upset about his "weakness," she was greatly relieved that his grumpiness was not a rejection of her, and expressed great sympathy about his work situation. Jack in turn felt greatly relieved that his fears and worries—and the irritability they produced—were understood.

Learning to say what was really on their minds was difficult for this couple, but it was essential to working out their sexual problems. They were able to discuss some of Jack's concerns about the future and plan some constructive steps, such as his going back to school two evenings a week, and they explored the possibility of Anne's taking a job when their youngest child graduated from high school the next year. Equally important, each of them began to express warmth and tenderness toward the partner, where before there had been only antagonism. We watched them become more affectionate from session to session. In the beginning they never really looked at each other. Gradually they began moving closer together, and eventually we saw them holding hands as they left our sessions—"like a couple of kids," they said, blushing.

Needless to say, this change affected their relationship in bed. Jack's anxiety about his professional future had found expression in anxiety about his potency. On several occasions he had been unable to get an erection. As they learned to share their feelings, each developed a better understanding of what the other was experiencing. Much of Jack's anxiety and tension abated, and he felt better about himself as a male, a sexual person. Anne, instead of withdrawing from him, began to reach out to touch and caress him, making no demand on him to perform—just enjoying the feeling of being close to him, of feeling loved. "I felt I had come home again after a long separation," she said.

YOUR PARTNER CAN'T READ YOUR MIND

One common block to communication is the implicit assumption that your mate should automatically know what you feel and want. It makes sense for an infant to trust his parents to discover and meet his needs—an infant has no way to express hunger, thirst, tiredness, or just wanting to be held. Many people carry this approach into adult life. They would like a particular response from their loved one, but they refuse to ask for it—and then are angry when they don't receive it. The only way to short-circuit this pattern is to realize that human beings are endowed with the capacity to communicate, but not with the ability to read each other's minds. If you want your partner to know how you feel or what you would like, you have to tell him or her directly.

We remember one young woman to whom we made the suggestion that she become more verbal about what she liked and didn't like in bed. "If you want your man to please you," we said, "you will have to show him what pleases you."

"But I don't like to have to tell him what I like; I want him to know. Having to tell him turns me off. I want him to be the ideal lover and my ideal lover knows what to do. Why does he have to be taught?"

We tried to correct this misconception:

> You are unique. Even if he had had a wide variety of women in his past and all the experience in the world, you would still be different from anyone else and you would still have to tell him what you like if you wanted him to know. Besides, your wants may change from one episode to another, from one moment to the next. Why should it be such a virtue not to have to ask? What could be sweeter, more ideal, than a lover who truly wanted to respond to the things you asked for?

You Can't Read Your Partner's Mind

One of the easiest ways to disrupt your communication with your partner is to assume you already know what he or she feels. Often one mate will say to the other, "I know how you feel—you don't have to tell me. You're angry—you're disappointed—you're upset."

There are two things wrong with telling your loved one what he or she feels. First, only that person can really know what he or she feels, just as only you can really know how you feel. Assuming you know someone's feelings when that person hasn't expressed them is a sure way to inject all kinds of misunderstanding and confusion into a relationship. Second, making yourself open to and accepting of what your partner has to say is itself a way of getting closer, entering an inner realm that your partner is letting you share.

Even people who have lived together for decades may totally misperceive each other's views. A middle-aged husband once told us privately, "I couldn't ask my wife to kiss my penis and put it in her mouth. I respect Sophie very much and I wouldn't want her to do anything that would offend her." When we asked how he knew it would offend her if they had never discussed it, he replied that anyone brought up in Sophie's generation would feel the same way. He was surprised when we told him that many women in Sophie's age group enjoyed oral sex and would not be offended by such a request. He would have been even more surprised had he heard Sophie tell us (without having heard her husband's discussion) that she would like him to stimulate her orally, that he had never attempted it and she therefore assumed the idea was distasteful to him. "I've always had the feeling he thought sex was somewhat dirty and I wouldn't want him to think of me that way. If it's ever going to happen, he'll have to initiate it and the odds are he never will."

The moral of this story is clear: find out from your partner what he or she wants; and don't assume you know until you ask and receive an answer.

THE ART OF OPENNESS

Openness to your loved one's intimate feelings is one of the greatest gifts you can bestow. But this is not a capacity that people are born with: it is a skill you can develop. Many people have the habit of closing up when others expose their inner lives because it makes them feel uncomfortable or anxious. By learning to identify these patterns, you can learn to break the ones you use.

One pattern is to engage in activities which may appear to be valid, but whose purpose is to enable you to avoid your mate's emotional expressions. A man may say, "I'm sorry, but I can't talk with you now; I've brought important paperwork home from the office that I have to work on." Or a woman may avoid her partner by keeping busy with housework or with the children when he indicates a desire to talk, or appears upset about something. Of course, such activities may indeed be necessary, but if there never seems to be a "right" time for intimate exchange, if it is always postponed, you can be pretty sure that you are using these activities as a means of avoidance.

Feeling Different Is All Right

Even if one partner listens to the other, the response may be one of criticism or attack, rather than acceptance. Dennis revealed to his wife that he usually felt uncomfortable at office parties because he felt socially inferior to most of the men present. Doris reacted by telling him, "That's ridiculous, that's what's wrong with you—you're always putting yourself down. No wonder you didn't get that promotion." In response, Dennis refused to discuss the matter further, even though Doris demanded that he do so. What had started as an attempt on Dennis's part to share a painful feeling, to reveal a part of himself he usually kept hidden, ended in an argument.

Melanie often acted cold and withdrawn when Fred's parents visited. "You treat them as if they were strangers," Fred shouted at her one evening after they had left. "Why can't you be more friendly?" When Fred described this incident to us he explained that it had ended with Melanie moving into the den for the night. He went on to say he had felt rejected by Melanie's treatment of his parents, and that feeling had been reinforced by her leaving the room. Afterward, he hadn't spoken to her for two days. Melanie tearfully explained that her behavior had nothing to do with Fred or his parents but his anger had made it impossible for her to share her feelings. She went on to explain that her own parents rarely responded to her letters and had never visited them since their marriage two years ago. The painful feelings stirred up by the visit of Fred's parents made it impossible for her to be warm and friendly to them.

If Fred had been able to ask Melanie why she acted the way she did in an attempt to understand her behavior, rather than criticizing her, it might have helped both of them feel closer, and the evening might have ended differently.

THE SELF-REPRESENTATION PRINCIPLE

Is there a way to establish channels of communication that bypass these barriers? We believe there is. We call it the principle of self-representation. Self-representation means taking responsibility for communicating what you feel and need and want, and letting your partner do the same. Once you learn how to do this, you can apply the same principle to relate more effectively to people in other areas of your life.

SPEAK FOR YOURSELF

The most important rule to follow in applying the principle of self-representation is to speak for yourself. This means saying "I" instead of "you." *I* feel angry, *I* feel upset,

I enjoy that. Talking in terms of "I" avoids blaming your partner or holding him or her responsible for the way you feel. Saying "You make me angry" or "You're hurting my feelings" implies that your partner set out to anger or upset you, which may not have been the case at all. And such a statement is likely to provoke a defensive reaction, perhaps a counterattack, and you're having another battle.

If your reaction to this idea of self-representation is, "I like this idea. I'd like to try it," why not present it in those terms to your partner? The chances are that the discussion will go better than if you ask, "What do you think of the idea?" without stating how you feel.

Again, talking in terms of *I* like, *I* need, *I* feel, involves some risk because your partner may respond with indifference or even rejection. However, in most relationships there is a degree of mutual concern and expressing your feelings and wishes is usually less risky than placing the responsibility for satisfying your feelings and needs on someone else.

THE "I" EXERCISE

We often recommend that couples try the "I" exercise as one way of improving their communication. These are the directions we give our patients; we suggest you and your loved one follow the same procedure.

For at least one week start every sentence with "I" instead of "you." Here are some pitfalls you should be aware of and try to avoid:

• Don't change "I" to "you" in the middle of the sentence. In other words, don't say, "I feel angry when you treat me that way." Say, "I feel angry. I would like to discuss it with you." Switching to "you" after an "I" statement continues to put responsibility for your feeling on your partner.

• Don't avoid talking in terms of "I" by asking questions ("What would you like to do tonight?"). Take responsibility for saying what you would like to do by saying, "I would like to go out to dinner. How does that sound to you?" In other words, express your wishes and solicit your partner's wishes. If the answer is, "No, I'd rather stay home tonight, but I'd like to eat out tomorrow," the chances are both of you will feel satisfied that a mutually acceptable decision has been negotiated.

• Don't avoid responsibility by saying, "It makes me furious." You're being much more direct if you can say, "I'm furious."

• Don't try to avoid responsibility by saying, "I don't care, anything you say is okay with me," or, "If that's what you want to do, I'm agreeable." Such abdication of responsibility paves the way for later resentment, particularly if your evening is a failure.

• Unless you've checked it out with your partner, don't talk in terms of "we": "We never seem to have fun any more" or "We used to feel much closer." Again, it assumes that you know what your partner is feeling.

I'D LIKE TO TRY THIS EXERCISE

Tell your mate how you feel about trying to talk in terms of "I" for at least one week. Find out how your mate feels. You might say to your partner, "I'd like you to help me with this. How about a signal when either one of us forgets 'I'?" Make a game of it and talk about how each one of you feels about the experience as the week progresses. The chances are you will try it for a longer time.

Many of our couples report that it made an important difference for them and served to improve their communication with each other and with other people as well.

A Simple Experiment

At times, couples see the point of the self-representation exercise at first. We remember one couple who felt very strongly that there was no conceivable benefit in it for them. "We've been married for twenty years; I know how she feels by now, and she knows how I feel." The man's wife agreed with him. They then decided that the best treatment for their sexual difficulties was a vacation, away from the pressures they were under. Several weeks later we had a card from them from Mexico.

When they came back from their vacation, they were barely on speaking terms. They had hoped their vacation would be an opportunity to enjoy their sex life, but they had quarreled a good deal while they were away. Bill began our next session by saying:

> You wouldn't believe the lousy time we had in Mexico. Call that a vacation? First of all, the food—you couldn't get a decent meal anywhere in fifty miles. Mexican food is all right once in a while, but not three meals a day all week. Second of all, the heat—it never got cool, even at night. And finally there was nothing to do but lie on the beach all day, no place you could even go to see a movie—I've never been so bored in all my life. I knew it wouldn't work out, but Sarah was so anxious to go I just went along with it.

At this point we interrupted his tirade:

> Now just a minute. Did you say where you wanted to go? Did you state your choice? Did you expect not to eat

Mexican food? You are blaming your wife, but the real problem is that you wouldn't say what you wanted—and now you're complaining because you didn't get it.

His wife, in tears, said:

You know, I really chose that place because I thought you'd like it—you talked a lot about doing something special this year. Actually, I wanted to see my relatives out West—but I knew you wouldn't enjoy that.

We commented:

It seems to us that neither of you can take responsibility for saying what you want. And the result, as you can see, is that neither of you gets what you would really like. Think how different it would have been if you, Bill, had said, "I'd like to go someplace where I can enjoy some excitement, good food and comfort." And you, Sarah, had said, "I'd like to visit my relatives out West." Maybe you'd have spent your vacation having a good time in San Francisco instead of quarreling on the beach in Mexico.

Neither of you was really trying to make yourself or your partner unhappy, but what you did had that result. Each of you needs to learn a different way to interact: you need to learn to say what *you* feel and what *you* want and to negotiate a decision together.

After repeating the basic philosophy of self-representation, we told them:

We want you to try a simple experiment. Why don't you plan a day that you would both enjoy and carry out our plan, following the rules for communication that we've suggested? See how much enjoyment both of you can get from it, and report back to us.

They laughed at themselves as Sarah described what had

happened when they followed our suggestion. They had agreed to do the planning part Thursday night.

After the dinner dishes were cleared, we sat down at the table, and Bill said, "Well, what would you like to do?" I said, "I don't know; why don't you decide this time?" We sat for a few moments, when suddenly Bill said, "Hey, we're doing it again. That is exactly what we were talking about with the doctors. So I guess I have to say something I'd really like to do. And I guess what I'd really enjoy is going out to the racetrack next Saturday afternoon."

"You would pick something you know I don't like," I said, "all that shouting, and cigar smoking and gambling."

"What's wrong with you," Bill replied, "is that you don't know how to enjoy a little excitement."

"Just a minute," I said. "We fell into the trap again. Now you're attacking me, instead of saying what you want. But I'm at fault, too. When you said you wanted to go to the track, I didn't say what I felt; instead I criticized you for what you wanted."

At this point, in an aside, Sarah said, "I suddenly began to see how we get into this same kind of trap each time." She then continued to recount their conversation:

I said, "All right, let me go back and start again. You want to go to the races. Well, I guess that isn't something I really enjoy. What I'd really like is—I'd really like to go to the flower show. You know I've wanted to go for the past three years, but somehow I've never made it out there in time."

"But now we're getting somewhere," Bill said. "Why don't we drive out next Saturday afternoon? I'll drop you at the flower show and drive over to the track. I can pick you up afterward, and how about a good steak dinner to finish off the day in style?"

"Now there's one thing we can agree on," I chimed in.

By the time they told us about their experience at their next session, they had not only learned a new way to interact, by expressing what they felt and wanted; they had also learned how to stop and laugh at themselves when they started to fall into the old patterns that came from ignoring the principle of speaking for yourself.

Representing yourself may also result in the realization that one or the other doesn't always have to compromise so that the couple can do something together. Although there is considerable enjoyment in sharing activities, the couple described above, like most couples, had special interests which they didn't share but enjoyed separately.

SAYING NO CAN BE O.K.

Communicating a refusal, particularly in the area of sex, can be interpreted as a rejection, which is often very painful. In some cases it may provoke anger. Yet everybody should be permitted to exercise the right to say no occasionally. One way to deal with a refusal is to link it to a future acceptance—"I feel tired tonight; I'd like to get some sleep so that we can have a really good session in the morning," or "I'm not feeling very sexual right now, let's just cuddle and we'll make love tomorrow night."

Of course, if either partner says no repeatedly, the reason has to be discussed and a mutual decision reached as to how to deal with the problem.

NONVERBAL COMMUNICATION

As we have indicated, verbalizing what you feel is tremendously important. But not all expression and communication is verbal. In intimate relationships, much of the most important communication is nonverbal. Kissing, touching, holding, looking, moving close, and moving away are all ways of expressing feeling. Such communication is often blocked by a virtual taboo on touching. Some children, especially girls, are often discouraged from touching themselves or enjoying their bodies. Others, especially boys, learn that giving and receiving physical affection is taboo. Many boys are brought up to believe that kissing and hugging, being touched and caressed, is somehow unmanly unless it leads to intercourse. Consequently, as adults many people have to redevelop the ability to be aware of and receptive to the full range of feelings they can experience in their bodies through touching, kissing, and caressing.

Closely related is the more general attitude of our society that no activity is worthwhile unless it has some definite objective. The pleasures of sensually touching and caressing your partner can't be fully experienced, however, if you think of them only as a means to achieve something else.

EXERCISE: "SENSATE FOCUS"
(Tuning in to Your Own Sensations)

We believe that all couples can benefit from giving themselves pleasure in a nondemanding, leisurely way. In this experience, to which Masters and Johnson gave the name "sensate focus," the only expectation should be to tune in to one's own sensations, to see what it feels like to touch and stroke and explore your partner's body, without having to concern yourself too much for the moment with your partner's reactions.

We're going to ask that you try this exercise at a time

when you're both in a good mood, relaxed, and have at least two hours of uninterrupted time at your disposal. You may not use all that time, but knowing you have the time will keep you from feeling pressured. If there are other people in the house, lock the door; if the telephone is apt to ring, take it off the hook.

The exercise should be embarked on with the clear understanding between you that it will *not* end in intercourse. Its purpose is not sexual but sensual, an opportunity to enjoy and rediscover the pure pleasure of touching.

Before you go any further, talk together about abstaining from intercourse on this occasion. Do you feel it is a deprivation or can you reach a mutual agreement to relax and enjoy yourselves, with no pressure on either side to perform?

What we're going to ask is that one of you invite the other into the bedroom. If the invitation is extended in the evening, the lights should be on, the bed coverings pulled down. You might begin by taking a bath or shower together. Try to forget your cares as you wash and pat each other dry before getting into bed nude.

One of you should then lie down on your stomach while the other begins to stroke and caress him or her. This exercise is devised for the giver, to concentrate on the pleasure and feelings he or she gets from touching and playing with the partner and giving pleasure without any concern about the partner's reaction. Let us tell you how we instructed one couple "to give to get":

> Betty, position yourself next to Sam, on his side or near his legs, just as long as you're comfortable and can reach out to touch and stroke and caress him all over.
> You might start with his back, stroking and rubbing him there for a few minutes. Then move up to his neck and head

—feel the shape of his head, the texture of his hair, the way it curls or falls straight. Play with his ears.

Now move back down his body. Trace the curves—go from the top of him, down his back, his waist. Feel the way his muscles bunch; feel where he's warm, where he's cool, where he's rough, where he's smooth. Apply different pressures as you move along his body caressing and exploring. See how it feels in the tips of your fingers, the palms of your hands, your forearm. Swish your hair over his body.

Don't concern yourself with Sam's reaction. The chances are Sam will like what you are doing. Betty, we want you to tune in to *your* feelings. We suggest that there be no talking during this exercise—it disturbs the mood. Sam, you can sigh or grunt or make whatever sounds you like, but no words. If you want to convey how much you like something you can move into it with your body. The only exception to the no-talking rule is that if the one on the receiving end feels any pain—from pinching or hard pressure—he can say ouch. You have the responsibility to protect your partner from hurting you. Otherwise, Sam, just lie on your stomach and enjoy it.

Betty, when you've finished stroking Sam's legs, the back of his ankles, even his toes, you might suggest that he turn over so you can begin caressing his face, tracing his features, going down toward his chest, his nipples, his abdomen, his thighs. On this particular occasion, we're going to suggest that you omit touching his penis and his testicles. Sexual arousal is not the purpose, it's a *sensual* experience.

Remember again, this exercise is for the toucher, to feel the sensations in her fingers, her hands, her elbows, as she gives her partner a total body caress. Experiment with different pressures, different rhythms.

When you have finished, Betty, you lie on your stomach, and now your only responsibility is to enjoy the sensations as Sam caresses you. Sam, now you do the same thing to Betty. You might begin in the same way, with her back, and move to her hair, feel the shape of her head, and proceed in the same way that Betty did, exploring her body, caressing her all over (except her breasts and genitals), perhaps learning something new about her or about yourself. Remember, focus on *your* sensations.

To enhance the experience we suggest you use a body lotion—even baby oil will do. What's important is that both of you like the texture and odor of the lotion. When using the liquid, pour it into a bowl—not directly on your partner's body. If the house is chilly, turn up the heat or put a heater near the bed. Warm the bottle of lotion under the faucet as you're preparing for bed.

Some of the questions people usually ask when we describe this exercise are:

• How long should I do this? As noted above, we recommend that you set aside two hours of unpressured time. Most couples spend twenty minutes to an hour for each person—but this is only a guide. If one partner feels tired or bored or satisfied, stop and let the other one take over. It's the quality of the exercise that counts, not the exact amount of time you spend doing it.

• What if I get aroused? Fine, but you don't have to do anything about it. Remember, we said no intercourse. However, if you should have an orgasm, that's fine too. This exercise doesn't usually end that way for most people.

• Some couples say it's not spontaneous. That may be so, but you'll find that most sexual and sensual enjoyment doesn't begin until you start caressing. So even if you're not in the mood when your partner invites you into the bedroom, don't refuse; you'll probably get into the mood after you begin.

If you've found the experience pleasurable, try it another time. Follow the same rules: Decide beforehand not to have intercourse. Take turns in initiating sensate focus. Pick the time that's right for you, morning, afternoon, or evening.

Vary the exercise by using your lips and tongue as part of the body caress.

Don't talk during the exercise but after share how you felt and what you liked. Betty described it as delightful. "I never realized how much I liked the long, sweeping strokes Sam used. And the lotion felt very sensual. The best part was just lying back and receiving—with no strings attached. I learned something new about Sam, too—that he enjoyed having his toes and his fingers caressed. We'd never done that before."

Sam had enjoyed the experience a lot too, but it had been hard for him to concentrate on his feelings. He found himself thinking about Betty and whether she was enjoying what he was doing, how he was touching her. But he admitted it felt good not to have any need to perform—just to enjoy what he was doing. And he discovered that his fingers and toes were a source of pleasure. When he caressed Betty, he learned how much she liked her back caressed and how good it was to spend time stroking the soft warm skin under her long hair.

Most people find this experience very relaxing and pleasurable, but this response is not universal. Some couples report they didn't get much out of the experience or that they felt a little anxious or uneasy at the idea of spending so much time concentrating on their own feelings. If the experience isn't a pleasurable one for you, try to figure out why. Talk about your reactions, why you were turned off or felt anxious. Sharing your feelings and reactions may serve to bring you closer and open up communication. You may learn new things about yourself and each other. Then try the exercise again; you may feel more relaxed the second time. Remember, focusing on your own pleasure isn't selfish. After all, the greatest pleasure you can give your partner is the knowledge that you're enjoying yourself.

Four

The Experience of a Lifetime

YOUR EXPECTATIONS

As a sexual occasion approaches, do you look forward to it with pleasure, expecting it to be deeply enjoyable and rewarding? Or do you approach it with misgivings, anticipating that it may be trying or even unpleasant?

There is a crucial relationship between your expectations about sex and your actual sex life. If you are expecting a relaxed, pleasurable experience, your whole being will prepare itself for full emotional and sexual response. If, on the contrary, you anticipate that sex will be something stressful, your mind and body will be on guard, poised to avoid any potential threat. Such an attitude not only interferes with your emotional state, it can disrupt your physiological responses as well. If on the other hand, you expect every sexual encounter to be an earth-shattering experience, you are bound to be disappointed.

Where do sexual expectations come from? They are deeply rooted in our early relationships, and are shaped by all our life experiences. In this chapter we will explore some common influences on our sexual selves. Try to reflect on what you brought from your past experiences and background to your present relationship. Because your expectations of love and intimacy often differ from those of your partner, it is helpful to examine not only your own background but that of your partner to arrive at a better and more realistic understanding of each other. We suggest that each of you read through this chapter separately and then share with each other what you have learned from it. We have included some questions along the way to assist you in your backward look. Some people find it helpful to talk over their past with a friend, a counselor, a therapist, to get a better perspective on how their life story has shaped their sexual attitudes and expectations.

THE BEGINNING OF LOVE

The very first experience we have with another human being is being touched. We learn about love and pleasure through being held, rocked, stroked, and caressed. Some baby animals die if the mother does not lick and stroke them. Even human babies sometimes do not survive if they are deprived of tender loving care. It was demonstrated in one study that children who were hospitalized because of illness and did not receive adequate cuddling and holding had a high death rate. When mothering was introduced, when the babies were picked up, played with, and tenderly administered to, the death rate fell dramatically.

A famous psychoanalyst, Erik Erikson, described this early period of life as the time when basic trust is established. If an infant's needs are met and he learns that he can count on another human being to be available to him, he grows up with the expectation that other people are to be trusted and counted on. The attachment he forms to his parents is the basis on which he forms loving attachments in the future.

Most of us don't remember our early infancy and toddler days; we have a kind of amnesia for that period. It's hard to recall how your parents held or fed or stroked or played with you. However, if you generally trust people and if you are able to form close and loving relationships, the chances are that in infancy your capacity to give and receive love got off to a good start. If you are excessively shy, mistrustful of people, frightened of becoming involved with others, it could be because, for one reason or another, you were deprived of some of the tender loving care we all need.

The basic trust and confidence developed in those early years influences the way we relate to our partner and the way we respond to our partner's caresses and touching. We never seem to outgrow our need for touching, perhaps because touching formed our very first bond with another human being.

Sometimes children experience touching as rough and heavy, and are likely to close themselves off to this pleasure in later life, just as a lack of basic trust in our parents can prevent becoming intimate with another person. We remember Leslie, a young woman who derived little pleasure from caressing, although she enjoyed intercourse and was frequently orgasmic. She described her husband's touch as heavy and felt that as a result she tightened up rather than relaxed when he touched her.

> I always felt my mother had a heavy hand. Although she meant to soothe and comfort me, her touch always made me curl up inside, as if somehow she was doing something wrong. I could never tell her that, any more than I can tell my husband I don't like his touch.

Eventually Leslie was able to deal with this, not with words but by guiding her husband's hand to show him the light, gentle strokes and the slow rhythm she preferred.

THE BEGINNING OF SEXUAL PLEASURE

Young children usually derive pleasure not only from the touch of their parents and others who care for them, but also from touching themselves. Just as they enjoy exploring the world around them, discovery of their own bodies is a fascinating activity even for very young children. They discover their fingers, their toes, their mouths, and their genitals. Such exploration sometimes leads to what appears to be an orgasm, although masturbation per se doesn't occur very often before nine or ten. Many parents find it difficult to accept the fact that this can occur, or that children come into this world as sexual beings. However, nurses and obstetricians will tell you that little baby boys are born with an erection and little baby girls lubricate within their first twenty-four hours. Sexuality is a birthright, but traditionally from the very beginning of life it has not been honored. For example, most small children are discouraged from touching their genitals. Sometimes parents do this unconsciously. A recent study showed this dramatically. Movies were made of parents caring for their young infants. Even parents who said they believed it was fine and natural for infants to play with their genitals were shown in the movies pulling their children's hands away from their genitals while they were being diapered. When the parents were shown the movies they were shocked at their own behavior. "I wouldn't believe I did it if I hadn't seen the movie with my own eyes," was the usual response. It seemed to demonstrate how deeply entrenched some of our sexual attitudes are.

The taboo on genital touching continues as children grow

older. It may take subtle forms; for example, parents may ask, "Do you need to go to the bathroom?" every time children touch their genitals. It may take the form of a direct prohibition. Children used to be threatened with dire consequences for such behavior. Such threats and prohibitions had a profound effect on sexual development, and were particularly apt to produce feelings of shame and guilt in regard to sex. Recently, these threats have diminished with the increased permissiveness and acceptance of sexual feelings, but the same unspoken message is still often conveyed to children.

It is not hard to see how such childhood experiences affect an individual's subsequent ability to relax and enjoy the natural expression of sexuality. If you learn that "Mother doesn't like you to touch yourself," genital pleasure or even the possibility of it is likely to make you a little anxious or uneasy years later. If you learn that everything connected with the genital region is dirty, touching, feeling, and thinking about your own or your partner's genitals is likely to give you an involuntary feeling of disgust. If you learn that sexual activity is something secret, part of you is likely to remain tense and on guard against discovery when you become sexually involved. More generally, the feeling that sex is somehow wrong, bad, dirty, and shameful is likely to make people block out the sexual sensations that come from the world around them and from their own bodies, even when as adults they think they would like to feel these sensations as fully and pleasurably as possible.

Warren exemplified the relationship between early experience and later attitudes toward sex. The first thing he said when we asked him about his sex life was:

> Have you read *Portnoy's Complaint*? That's my story. I was the pride and joy of my parents, the family opportunity to become somebody, the center of my parents' life.

I was watched over like a plant, tended, watered, given the best place in that small universe. But what nobody knew about was what I did behind locked doors, or under the covers at night. I found out about masturbating when I was in the eighth grade and spent a weekend with a friend. He couldn't believe I hadn't jerked off before. Well, it was the beginning of a long career. My mind rejected the idea because it was such a secret activity. I always worried about being caught. I felt ashamed to be doing something that I seemed to have no control over—it controlled me.

Nobody ever did catch me, but once my father gave me a lecture on the subject; he must have suspected what I was doing. At times, I was sure he could see right through the walls. He didn't tell me I'd go crazy or anything like that. He just lectured me on how some boys just couldn't control themselves and got into trouble, throwing away their opportunities. He preached that sex was something someone with willpower could put aside until the proper time. Of course, he didn't say when that was. I kind of wondered if he had ever found the proper time. It made me feel guilty and ashamed that I couldn't put it aside.

I never talked with anyone about it until I was years older. I never felt good about masturbating; I still don't, even though I should know better. I still feel ashamed that I masturbate from time to time now, even though I have a good sex life with my wife. Of course, she doesn't know about it and that makes me feel even more ashamed. The funny part of it is that some of the same old guilt and shame has always been connected with anything sexual I've done from the first time I made it with a girl to making love to my wife. I feel I have to make up to her in other ways for being so interested in it and wanting it, even though my rational mind knows that she's as interested in it as I am and wants it too.

When Warren eventually confided to his wife that he occasionally masturbated, her first reaction was amazement that Warren had indulged in this activity without her knowledge, although they had been sharing the same bed for years. Actually, Warren had always been careful to wait until she was asleep. And this had only increased his guilty feelings, which was the chief reason he decided to tell his wife; he would then be able to masturbate without fear of discovery. His wife's next reaction was that she must be doing something wrong or why would he need to masturbate? After all, she was supposed to satisfy all his needs. Although this is an almost universal reaction of women, the fact is that many men and women masturbate either occasionally or regularly even though they have enjoyable sex lives with their partners.

LEARNING ABOUT SEX

Growing children, who are actively involved in an effort to understand their world, are often intensely curious about sex. All too often, however, this curiosity is deflected: their questions about sex are answered evasively; their efforts to discover sexual information for themselves are discouraged or, if possible, circumvented by parents, teachers, and other adults. Children may notice a general embarrassment when any sexual subject arises. When they ask questions about sex, they are likely to sense their parents' discomfort in talking about it, or notice that their parents suppress a laugh or a smirk. In one way or another, children pick up the message all too clearly: learning about sex is both exciting and restricted. They learn to feel anxious in the face of discussions of sex, or even the exchange of ideas that have sexual connotations. Most children don't have a model to whom they can talk about sex comfortably. As a result, talking about sex is always fraught with some anxiety.

On the surface, postponing the acquisition of sexual knowledge until a later age might appear to be harmless.

But its effects on the child's development may be insidious: It teaches them to suppress their curiosity about sex, to avert their attention, to block out sexual information when it does become available.

From the various bits of information and misinformation they receive, the results of their own explorations, and their feelings and fantasies, children piece together a conception of sexuality that may stay with them long after they have left the world of childhood behind.

> A sixty-year-old woman told us that as a youngster she was convinced she would become pregnant if a boy kissed her. Even though she learned the facts of life (from books) when she was older, she found it difficult to give up her misconceptions because of her early conditioning. For example, her mother had never discussed sex with her, had never even mentioned menstruation, had never showed her husband any physical affection. And our patient had adopted the same prudish attitudes. She found it impossible to talk about sex or be demonstrative to her husband.

Perhaps the best sex education for children comes from an opportunity to observe their parents' loving relationship. If parents are warm and affectionate with each other, their children will get a lasting impression of the pleasures involved in a relationship between a man and a woman. If parents are cold, distant, or unresponsive to each other, their children will have a poor model for a loving relationship between adult partners. One patient told us, "I never saw my parents even hold hands. They must have had sex because I'm here, but if you lived in our house you wouldn't think there was such a thing as sex in the world." Almost invariably, children learn to imitate such attitudes of physical defensiveness and distancing, and as adults find themselves applying them toward their own partners.

In addition, specific experiences may give children negative views and expectations about sex. Quite frequently children observe or overhear their parents making love. If they have not learned that sex is a natural and enjoyable part of life, they are likely to misinterpret what they see or hear as something violent and disturbing. Children may have sexual advances of one kind or another made to them by disturbed adults. Upsetting as these may be in themselves, the distress is often aggravated by their parents' hysterical reactions to such disclosures. Some parents, on the other hand, try to deny that the incidents ever occurred, which confuses children, making them doubt themselves and their perceptions. Finally, women of any age may be subject to rape. Such violent sexual attacks almost inevitably leave women with fears about sex, fears about men, and negative feelings about their own sexuality.

CHILDHOOD PLAY

As children mature, their relationships with other children take on an added dimension. Often they include exciting pleasures as cuddling, looking, and touching. Such sexual play is a normal and pleasurable part of growing up for most children.

Yet, young children caught engaging in sex play are likely to be sternly rebuked. Many people have memories of sexual games that were discovered by shocked adults who reacted as if they had committed some crime. Sometimes the word is spread among neighborhood parents, who forbid their children to play with the supposed perpetrator. Ironically, often the children involved don't even understand what they were doing that was bad, but the reaction of the discovering adults leaves its mark. However, not all parents react in this negative way. One man told us:

> When I was ten years old, there was a skinny little girl next door. We examined each other and she said, "Let's do it." I didn't know what "doing it" meant, but she showed me. I was pretty upset about it, and told my parents. Fortunately, they took it in stride, and even bought some books for me to read about sex. For a while I read like crazy, trying to put it all together, but after a while I kind of lost interest and went on to other things.

As children reach the preteen years, they also frequently become "best friends" with other children of their own age. In our society, these preadolescent "chum" relationships are most common between members of the same sex. They are often another important step in developing the capacity for mature relationships. With these close friends children can learn how to look at the world from another's point of view and learn to care deeply for a person outside of the family. Such friendships help children learn to combine dependence and independence in a relationship between equals, and are steppingstones to more mature relationships.

Miriam recalled sleeping over at her best friend's house when she was about twelve. They shared the same bed and would talk and giggle throughout most of the night.

> We'd compare the size of our breasts, the amount of pubic hair in the "forest," as we used to call it, and then suddenly, we were touching each other's breasts and it felt good. It was a scary feeling because I knew we were doing something we shouldn't be doing, but I looked forward to those sleepovers. One night, Elsie's hand was between my legs and I thought I was going to explode. It wasn't until years later I realized I'd had an orgasm. We never had another sleepover after that night. I just told Elsie I thought

I had outgrown them, and she agreed and it was around that time that we began dating. After that, I never had a close girl friend. I guess I was afraid I might become a lesbian.

Guilt about such experiences often persists for many years because most young people are unaware that some same-sex play is a common experience.

LOOKING BACK—EARLY CHILDHOOD

How would you describe your family life when you were little? What were your mother and father like? What kind of relationship would you say they had? Were they affectionate with each other? With you? What impression did you have as to which parent was in charge—who ran the show, so to speak? Did you have brothers and sisters? Were they older or younger than you? How did you get along together? Were you particularly close to one of them? Do you feel that either one or both of your parents had a favorite? Was it you?

Were there other important adults in your life? Grandparents, a maid, an aunt or uncle? Did you feel lonely as a child, left out of things? Did your mother work outside of the house? If so, how did you feel about it? Who took care of you? Did your father spend much time with the family? What did your father do? Were your parents in comfortable circumstances? Did you feel deprived, unable to get things you wanted or others had?

Were your parents religious? What role did religion play in your life? What attitudes about sex and marriage did you develop as a result of your religious training? How do they affect you now?

How did you learn about intercourse? What was your reaction? Did you talk with your friends? Do you remember any sexual experiences with them, or way back, when you were very little, playing doctor? With whom? Were you ever caught? Punished? When did you first discover that it was pleasurable to touch your genitals? Were you ever warned against this? Did you engage in it often? Reach a climax? What were your feelings about it?

ADOLESCENCE

Toward the beginning of the second decade of life, certain areas of the brain trigger release of the hormones which bring about puberty. The age at which this occurs differs by several years from individual to individual; it averages about a year earlier for girls than for boys. It leads to a rapid spurt of growth, a zooming interest in sex, and the emergence of the male and female secondary sexual characteristics.

In boys, the onset of puberty is signaled by the growth of body hair on the face, around the penis, and under the arms, lowering of the voice, deepening of the chest, and the manifestation of other characteristics of adult males. One of these characteristics is that orgasms are accompanied by the ejaculation of semen. Boys generally discover this either through masturbation or through nocturnal emissions—wet dreams. Although they may be made to feel guilty about it, almost all boys proceed to have orgasms frequently through adolescence, whether through masturbation, wet dreams, petting, or intercourse.

In girls, puberty is likewise marked by the development of adult female characteristics. Pubic hair grows, breasts begin to swell, and the body eventually assumes a more rounded form. Most dramatically of all, ovulation and menstruation begin, and, after a period of irregularity, occur in a regular monthly cycle. The amount of sexual activity and interest begins to rise, but in our society, at least, this increase is considerably more gradual for most girls than for most boys, although this may be changing.

The physical, psychological, and social changes of adolescence are often somewhat distressing. Many girls are poorly prepared for the onset of menstruation and find it an unpleasant or even frightening experience. Many boys and girls feel intensely self-conscious about their physical attractiveness, because their features grow at uneven rates during these growth spurts. Often the negative body image developed during this period hangs on for many years.

In addition, adolescents are subjected to a whole new barrage of admonitions about sex, most of them directed toward the dangers of sexual intercourse. They are warned frequently of the dangers of venereal disease and pregnancy, but rarely given reliable information as to the prevention of these "disasters." In strict, religious families the children may be solemnly and repeatedly warned that premarital sex is a sin. As a result of these admonitions, adolescent sexual activity is likely to become surrounded by an aura of guilt and shame.

Negative attitudes toward sex can affect even those who appear "sexually liberated," who engage in sexual activities despite the prohibitions against them. Sylvia, a very pretty, vivacious young woman, had been having intercourse since her sophomore year at high school. She felt that in a way her behavior reflected a rebelliousness toward her parents more than any great sexual desire on her part. Of course, Sylvia's parents didn't know about it, but it gave her a kind of secret pleasure that she was doing something they would strongly disapprove of.

Sylvia described her mother as "the guardian of my virginity."

When I was a kid, she began to warn me about boys—how they were only after one thing and that a girl had to be careful or she'd get pregnant. I guess part of it was that I was sort of a wild kid, staying out late, going to lots of parties, having a lot of friends. My mother thought sex was a big part of it, though it really wasn't at all. The main thing was being part of the crowd. We did a lot—danced and went bowling and just sat around and smoked. Of course there was some fooling around and some of the kids were into heavy sex but they drifted away from the crowd. My mother always sat up and waited for me—when I came in, I used to think she thought she could tell by looking at me what I had been doing. She always had opinions about the boys I went with and they didn't always coincide with mine.

Now that I look back at it I think my mother thought I'd get into trouble and marry young. She and my father had married in their late teens and she didn't want that to happen to me. She wanted me to go to college and have a fuller life than she did. Well, I did go to college and fulfilled her ambitions in that way. But I'm afraid I've also lived out her admonition to be careful. I just can't seem to let go sexually. I've tried hard enough, with a number of partners, but somehow I get to a certain point and it's as if something clicks off. And though I've tried to be freer it's as if something restrains me—an inner voice saying, "Sylvia, put the brakes on; don't you see the red light ahead?" If I have oral sex, it's the same thing, so it's not the old warning "You'll get pregnant," but the whole feeling you're doing something you shouldn't. Once in a while, something cracks through and I feel a lot of pleasure, so I know there's nothing really wrong with me, but I do have a lot of hang-ups about enjoying myself sexually.

Boys are subject to a different set of inhibitions. Their

behavior is governed by two fears that are frequently inter-
twined: one, that they are not aggressive enough to "make"
it in a competitive world; and two, that they may become
homosexual. These fears often lead to a general fear of
touching, of tenderness, or of anything else that might be
interpreted as "weak," or "feminine." Gentleness is avoided.
Needs for dependence, for being held and comforted, are
repressed. Thus a vast realm of sensual and emotional experience is cut off.

For adolescent boys the pleasure of sex does not lie in the
activity itself or in the relationship to one's partner, but in
what you can brag about to the boys tomorrow. Those who
do not do well in this sexual competition often feel they are
inadequate, and envy what they may envision as other boys'
"techniques" for "success" with girls. On the other hand,
those who are "successful" may emerge with attitudes which
make sex primarily a test of their masculinity.

Lucy was married to just such a man:

> Ralph isn't satisfied unless I have an orgasm every time.
> But just his anxiety makes me turn off. After all, I can't
> always produce an orgasm just to please him. I try, but the
> pressure on me is too great. I find myself angry at Ralph
> and not wanting to have sex a lot of the time.

Ralph described his hurt and confusion. It was apparent
that he cared for Lucy very much, and he showed this concern and consideration in every way. He seemed to take it
for granted that we would understand that he wanted to
please her sexually and would approve of his willingness to
put considerable effort into "making her come."

As we talked further, Ralph revealed that in addition to
wanting to satisfy Lucy, he felt that it was a man's responsibility to bring his partner to an orgasm; doing it was like

getting some kind of award. This reminded him that when he was in high school some of the boys used to kid about getting a merit badge for how many girls they "laid."

> At that point, I hadn't laid any girl, just dreamt about it and made a few futile attempts, but I didn't admit that. A few years later at college, I got in with a group who used to cruise around picking up girls, and we'd compare notes as to whether we'd scored. Nobody ever talked about whether you liked the girl—it was all performance. Maybe it's different now—this was back in the forties.

When he met Lucy in his senior year, she was the first girl he ever really cared about.

> I didn't care if I never slept with another girl. But I guess the measure of the man for me shifted from numbers to making Lucy happy. Just as I started out by proving how fast I could get a girl to bed, so it became almost an obsession to prove to Lucy how good a lover I was, and what better proof was there than for me to bring her to orgasm?

To change the situation, Ralph and Lucy began to discuss with each other their wishes, needs, and desires. They spent a lot of time together, camping, going to concerts, and in other enjoyable pursuits. When they developed a closer, more loving relationship, it was easier for them to communicate their likes and dislikes more specifically during sexual encounters. Lucy made it clear that to be held closely and to be touched tenderly was more important than for Ralph to strive to "make her come."

Despite some of the conflicts and turmoil during this period, adolescence is also a time of exciting discovery of one's potential in many areas of development. The sexual area receives considerable attention, and experimentation involves kissing, hugging, genital play, mutual masturbation, and often the first attempt at intercourse. Attachment to a particular individual is a frequent consequence of sexual play and almost all adolescents fall in love and maintain a continuing relationship for varying periods of time. Going steady, or going together, is an important and valuable preparation for later commitment to a more long-lasting relationship.

Looking Back—Adolescence

Was adolescence a difficult time for you? What were some of the problems? The joys? Did you have any special friends? Girls? Boys? When did you start dating? Did you go steady? Did you feel lonely? Were you part of a group in high school?

When did you reach puberty? Begin to menstruate? Were you prepared beforehand? What was your reaction? How do you feel about menstruation now?

When did you first start "making out"? When did you have your first experience with being nude, touching genitals? Were you excited? Did you come?

What about masturbation? How old were you when you first began to masturbate? When did you first masturbate to orgasm? Do you remember the fantasies that accompanied masturbation then? How often do you masturbate now? If you haven't masturbated in recent years, or have never masturbated, what do you think has restrained you? Would you like to learn to masturbate?

Do you recall when you first began to notice changes in your body? How did you feel? Were you concerned about the size of your breasts? Did you feel your penis was too small? Did you talk with anyone about your feelings? Did you feel you were sexually attractive? Do you now? Are you satisfied with the way you look, your weight? Do you feel your partner finds you attractive? Do you feel comfortable being nude—by yourself, with your partner? Do you go to bed nude?

When was the first time you had intercourse? With whom? What was the situation; and how did you feel about it? Did you find it pleasurable? What about contraception? With how many partners have you had intercourse? What were the different experiences like for you? What did you learn from them about yourself, about your needs? If you didn't have intercourse before marriage, what held you back—your value system, your fears, the unavailability of a partner?

ADULTHOOD AND MARRIAGE: THE EARLY YEARS

Today, many unmarried couples live together for months or years. In most cases, however, if such arrangements last, they usually lead to marriage eventually. According to current statistics, 90 percent of all people in our society get married. (Although many marriages end in divorce, most divorced people remarry sooner or later.) Thus, for most adults, sexual activity occurs primarily within the framework of marriage.

Many couples who did not have intercourse before marriage report their honeymoon was a "disaster." Sometimes the partners literally did not know what to do, or they may have avoided the sexual "moment of truth." ("He stayed up all night watching TV instead of coming to bed.") It would be amazing if such problems did not arise when people are poorly prepared for sexual activity. Unfortunately, however, these first experiences with intercourse can often set the pattern for future sexual encounters.

Mildred and Henry exemplified the effects of a traumatic first experience. When we first met them they had been married for two years, both of them miserable as far as sex was concerned. The main problem, according to Henry, was Mildred's "nervousness." "It's as if she expects pain rather than pleasure." It had gotten so Henry didn't even feel like making love to his wife and was seriously considering leaving her; his resentment about sex colored his whole attitude toward their marriage.

Mildred told us,

I can't help it; I just don't enjoy it. In a way I almost dread it because I know it won't be good. What upsets me about the whole thing is that I went into marriage looking forward to sexual relations, because I was very attracted to my husband. We didn't have intercourse before we got married—that was how we wanted it—but I didn't think I had any hang-ups. We petted a lot and I enjoyed it. I think the problem started on our wedding night. We tried intercourse and it didn't work out. Henry had an erection but I was too tight or nervous. I don't know. We kept trying; I didn't know what was wrong, but he couldn't penetrate. I remember crying a lot and telling him to "do something." I resented that he couldn't solve the problem, even though I recognized that there was something wrong with me.

The honeymoon was a nightmare as a result of what was not happening in the bedroom, and I couldn't wait to get home. I went to a gynecologist who stretched my hymen under anesthesia. That only seemed to make things worse. We both felt even more inadequate. Eventually we did have intercourse, but I think of our bedroom as the last place I want to be. I'm always nervous and I guess Henry is fed up with trying to make me enjoy it. Our whole relationship has been spoiled by it. I don't want Henry to leave. I really love him very much.

Fortunately this couple was willing to make a "second start." Mildred had a condition known as vaginismus, which means that she involuntarily tightened her vaginal muscles and therefore narrowed the vaginal opening. This makes intercourse uncomfortable and sometimes impossible. Mildred and Henry were urged not to have intercourse for a while, but rather to go back to the pleasurable noncoital activities of their courtship days. In addition, Mildred was taught how to relax her vaginal muscles and was given specific suggestions as to how to stretch her vagina so that eventually intercourse became more pleasurable for her, and Henry's confidence in his sexuality increased. He confided that he had feared he was becoming impotent.

A loving relationship with one's sexual partner can of course do much to overcome the blocks to sexual expression that developed earlier. But difficulties, tensions, and hostilities in marriage can also do much to disrupt good sexual functioning.

Some of these difficulties result from the realistic problems of daily life. Couples are almost bound to come into conflict at times over finances and life-style. In a time of changing sex roles, they are likely to have somewhat different expectations of who should be responsible for what. They may have differences over whether to have children, how many, and how to handle them.

Life With Children

Pregnancy and childbirth enhance feelings of closeness. But they can also add tension and strain to a relationship, and have a negative effect on sexual activity, although there is nothing inherent in these conditions to interfere in any major way with a good sex life. Contraception can become an issue between a couple, although the option to prevent conception is probably one of the greatest contributions to sexual pleasure.

Studies show that the early years of child rearing provide the greatest strain on the marital bond. It is reassuring to know that most new parents go through considerable turmoil, and that this is a time of considerable stress even for so-called normal, happy couples.

Dedicating yourself to the care and demands of a family of young children and at the same time giving attention to an intimate relationship with your partner requires a delicate balance. This dilemma is even further complicated today by dual careers and changing sex-role expectations. The sexual relationship of most couples seems to suffer during this period of life because of exhaustion from the stresses and strains of everyday living. Fortunately, babies and young children also bring joy and fulfillment to a couple to help them weather this transition to parenthood. Also, experts recommend that the most important aid couples have to sustain their relationship is to talk over together what they are feeling. Understanding what is happening, sharing anticipations about the future, and, above all, setting time aside for each other can make this period one of growth rather than of deterioration of the marriage.

Besides the stresses and strains of daily life, many sources of hostility and detachment in sexual relationships are more psychological in nature. For example, often people carry over from childhood the belief that it is the responsibility of their partner to meet their needs, just as their parents did when they were small children. If their mate fails to do so, they feel mistreated and angry. Or one or both partners may define their relationship as a power struggle, a

struggle usually derived from factors in their original families. Once partners see each other as rivals, their sex lives
may become a battleground, their sexual responses or lack
of them pawns in the battle.

MARRIAGE IN MIDDLE AGE

This is often referred to as the empty-nest period of life,
because children leave home to make lives of their own.
For the first time in many years husband and wife are alone
together again and need to adjust to a new relationship. For
some the adjustment is difficult because children have been
the only bond between them, and in a sense provided a safe
way to avoid direct involvement with each other. If they
think their productive years are over, one or both partners
may feel sadness or disappointment at their lack of achievement. If goals have been reached, questions may arise as to
whether it was worth all the struggle. Menopause and health
problems may restrict activity and cause concern. Fear of
aging and dying may produce considerable anxiety. All of
this may result in less social and sexual activity and a feeling
of isolation from each other.

But for others this period is one of liberation. Couples
turn to each other to fill the gap left by the children and feel
a renewed sense of romance and support from each other.
With the life span longer than ever before in history, and
most middle-aged couples in better health than in previous
generations, many couples renew their interest in life. Since
some feel the sexual revolution passed them by, there is a
new interest in enriching their sexual life before it is too
late. Women, particularly, freed from homemaking responsibilities, have an opportunity to pursue new interests and
careers.

Looking back on the early years of marriage and forward to the years ahead, we realize that we bring to marriage a lifetime of expectations, fears, hopes, strengths, and weaknesses that can be traced back to our very first years of life. The society within which we grew up also has a profound effect on our psychosexual and psychosocial development from which many of our attitudes originate. Add all this to the complexities of interacting with a partner who has his or her own complex history and add, too, that we are living in an era of rapidly changing mores, and it becomes clearer why some people question how the institution of marriage can endure. Yet, the statistics given above indicate that most people seem to feel there is no substitute yet devised for the close, intimate relationship marriage provides for husband, wife, and children. Divorce usually ends in remarriage and is for many a way of trying to find the intimacy which they failed to find in the first marriage. Unfortunately, divorce often causes considerable trauma, particularly for children.

Whatever the difficulties, most people find sex most satisfying within the context of marriage or other lasting, committed relationships, for these allow a development of mutual knowledge and understanding that can arise in no other way. With patience, love, and understanding, many sexual difficulties can be overcome. Indeed, studies reveal that most married couples report that sex grows increasingly satisfying as the years pass.

MARRIAGE: LOOKING BACK AND TO THE FUTURE

How did you first meet your present partner? How old were you? Do you recall your first impression of him/her? What attracted you most? Does that still hold today? What made you decide to get married? Whose idea was it? Do you have any regrets? What were your expectations about sex and lovemaking before you got married? Do you think they have been fulfilled for the most part? What are some of your disappointments in lovemaking; in marriage generally?

Did you have a wedding, a honeymoon? What were they like for you? Did you have sex together before your honeymoon—with your husband, with other partners? Was it different before and after marriage? What made it different—better, worse, more frequent, less frequent? Are you satisfied with the frequency now? Do you think your partner is? Who usually initiates lovemaking? Does it always lead to intercourse? What do you find most stimulating, what turns you off?

Do you tell your partner what pleases you most? Do you show him/her how to please you? Do you know enough about yourself to be able to communicate your needs to your partner?

What, if any, birth control method do you use? Do you both feel satisfied with the method? Does one or the other of you feel resentful about assuming all the responsibility for birth control? Would you like to change to another method? Have you considered a vasectomy, or female sterilization?

Do you have children? Were they planned? Do you want more children? Would either or both of you prefer to remain childless? Is this an issue between you?

What was pregnancy and childbirth like for each of you? Did it affect your sex life? Was your child nursed? Did you enjoy that—both of you? Were you together during childbirth? What was that like? Would you want to be together next time?

Has the presence of small children had a disruptive effect on your relationship in general—on your sex life in particular? Do you feel tired, pressured, unable to relate to each other intimately? Is saying no a problem for either of you?

Many people engage in sexual activities that do not involve their partners—masturbation or extramarital affairs—what about you? If you do, is your partner aware of it? Have you ever discussed either of these two activities? Ever masturbated in front of each other? Ever fantasized other partners? In what way do you think your marriage has been affected if there have been partners outside the marriage?

If yours is a marriage in the middle years, has it improved or deteriorated with the passage of time? With lessened responsibility for child care, is your time hanging heavy on your hands? Are you working? Do you feel close to your partner, or does the empty nest confront you and does your partner seem like a stranger? What about your sex life?

As you look ahead to the future, what are some of your fears, your hopes? What are your views about sexuality in the later years?

Five

What You and Your Partner Want and Need

YOUR UNIQUE SEXUALITY

We made the point earlier that your sexual needs, feelings, and desires are unique. They grow out of your personal anatomy and physiology, the attitudes of your parents and friends while you were growing up, your past experiences, your relationship with your partner, and your sexual expectations. The same is true for your partner. One of the keys to a good sexual relationship is to develop a real knowledge and understanding of your partner's sexuality, and to help your partner become familiar with all aspects of you as a sexual person. Knowledge of your partner's sexual history helps to explain many of his or her reactions that appear to be illogical or unreasonable.

PRIVACY AND SHARING

As you look back on your personal and sexual history, you and your partner will probably each have some thoughts about your sexual past, present, and future. Some of these reflections you will no doubt want to keep to yourself. Almost everyone has at least a few things he or she doesn't want to tell anyone. We believe firmly that privacy is a basic right. And respecting that privacy can play a positive role in a relationship. Both partners must recognize that each is an independent person with his or her own world, which need not always be identical with the world they share. An insistence on "total honesty," or "calling a spade a spade," in which every passing thought, feeling, and experience must be exposed to another's examination, can often be a cover for the wish to attack and control one's mate. A respect for privacy, on the other hand, means that what *is* shared is shared freely, as a gift. In this way privacy and sharing are mutually dependent. So by all means feel free not to tell your partner those reflections on your sexuality or your sexual experience that you don't want to share, and respect your loved one's freedom not to reveal all.

Jeffrey told us of an experience he had during his college years which he found difficult to talk about with his wife. He wasn't sure she'd understand.

I find it hard to believe myself sometimes. I'm pretty sure I'm not a homosexual—I've never had any other experiences in the years since—but I can remember to this day how turned on I was to this guy. My roommate had gone away for the weekend and a friend of his was staying in our room. We liked each other right away and spent hours talking. He didn't know anybody on campus—he had come to look the place over. It was a bad night—cold and wet and I had some food so we ate in the room—we had some beer and suddenly my head was in his lap and he was stroking my hair. I got really excited and, well, what happened seemed so natural at the time I didn't give it a second thought, but I've had trouble not thinking about it ever since. I don't think I'd want Jenny to know.

Jeffrey was surprised to hear that Kinsey's data showed that 50 percent of the men in his survey have a homosexual experience that ends in ejaculation sometime in their life, but his wish not to share this experience with his wife was respected.

Sandra's problem was more complicated. Sandra thought that she was lucky as a child because her parents were very open about sex and she always felt free to come to them with her questions. Her house had always been open to her friends and she was envied by them because she was not subject to as many rules and regulations as they were. Sandra had a particularly close attachment to her mother, who was a lawyer and received considerable recognition for her achievements. Her father seemed to take second place in their large circle of friends, but was a very successful businessman and highly respected. Sandra never felt as close to him as she did to her mother, probably, she thought, because he was absent from home a good deal because of his work. When Sandra was about fourteen, just about the time she began dating, she discovered that her mother had been having an affair for several years with one of her father's partners.

> It plunged me into a premature sex life. It was as if my mother had given me permission to do anything I wanted to do. I gave up my ambition to be a lawyer like she was and instead emulated her in her secret behavior. I began sleeping with Tom, before my fifteenth birthday. He was a few years older and sensible enough to use birth control. We used to meet after school in his house. My mother never found out about it and I sort of felt proud that I, too, had a secret sex life.
>
> After high school I had a few romances, but most of my energy went into working hard and getting training as a sculptor. Jim and I have been married for four years. He's an artist too and we have a wonderful life together but I

find myself involved with another man sexually right now—a friend of Jim's—and it's as if I'm right back to wanting a secret sex life. I think if I told Jim about it he would leave me. I don't want that to happen so I've decided to go for help with this problem so I can preserve our marriage.

In Sandra's case, psychotherapy was a wise choice to help her avoid repeated involvement in similar situations.

In addition to the things you would like to keep private, there are probably some things you would like to share with each other. These may range from casual memories that you had forgotten and know that your mate would enjoy, to profound insights that you feel might make a basic change in your love life, to things you have always wished your partner knew but didn't know how to talk about. The purpose of the next exercise is to give you and your mate an opportunity to tell each other about reflections on your background and expectations that you want to share.

EXERCISE: FILLING EACH OTHER IN

Read through this exercise separately and see what points it raises that you want to go into with your partner. You may also want to give more time to thinking about your past and how it has affected your sexual attitudes and behavior. You may want to jot down a list of things you want to tell your partner about.

Now make a date to discuss them. Remember, it is your responsibility to help your mate understand your sexuality, to share what you want to share of your past experiences, present feelings, and hopes for the future. And it is also your job to really listen to your partner, to try to understand his or her background, and find out if there are ways you can be helpful.

Finally, remember the rules of self-representation:

- *Don't* try to read your partner's mind. Ask about what you want to know. Don't assume you know.
- *Don't* criticize or attack your partner.
- *Do* say what you yourself feel. Use "I" to represent your thoughts, feelings and desires.

Here are some things you may want to tell your partner about:

Expectations

Are there expectations you have about sex and marriage which you think you would like your partner to know? Tell your loved one about them. You can start with the experiences that they grew out of. Explain how you felt about them at the time, and how you feel about them now. Discuss whether you want to change them. And tell your partner specifically if there are any ways he or she could be of help.

EXERCISE: SHARING EXPECTATIONS

Unless you make your expectations clear, your partner has no way of knowing what they are. Nor can you know what your partner's expectations are. Even more important, unless there is this kind of communication there may be no way of finding out whether your expectations mesh or if there's a wide discrepancy between them.

As part of your attempt to get some perspective on the relationship of your past to your present, write down a list of five things you expect from your partner. Ask your partner to do the same. Before you exchange lists ask yourself where these expectations come from. Ask yourself if they are realistic in terms of the present. Do you think your mate is capable and willing to meet these expectations?

Exchange lists and study your reactions to your partner's list. Do you feel willing and able to meet what he wants? Do you feel his expectations are realistic in the present situation? Talk over your expectations and your reactions to your partner's expectations. Are you trying to change your partner to meet your expectations, or is there a need to change yourself?

One thing Betty had put on her list was that she expected Bob to be more dependable. She found his irregular hours disturbing and often suspected him of being interested in another woman because he was away from home so much. Bob, on the other hand, resented Betty's nagging him about this and her desire that he help her more at home. He wrote that he expected understanding and support in light of his demanding career. As they discussed this particular issue between them Betty realized that her anxiety was connected with her father's behavior rather than Bob's. Her father had been an alcoholic and often stayed away from home for days at a time. He eventually deserted his wife and children for another woman. Betty wanted a man she could depend on; because of Bob's irregular hours her old anxiety about her father's absence from home was stirred up. Her concern about dependability did not relate to Bob at all. Bob, on the other hand, expected the kind of complete understanding of his work and schedule that his parents had always given him. An electrical wizard from an early age, he had always been treated as very special and no demands were made on him at home to report on his comings or goings or to help around the house. He was, however, very dependable in all other respects.

Bob and Betty both realized, on the basis of their better understanding of each other, that each of them needed to change somewhat rather than expecting all the change from the other.

Things You Want Your Partner to Know

Are there things about your past that would make you more comfortable for your partner to know? Things that you've had on your mind from time to time but have never found the right occasion to bring up? This is an opportunity to raise them.

Don't use this time to bring up past grievances against your partner. Reciting all the dissatisfactions of the past can only drive a couple apart. Think in terms of the way the past can help you to understand yourself better or help your partner to understand you better.

> One of the things Daryl had been reminded of in going over his background was that he had had a period of impotence for several months during his first marriage. It had shaken him greatly at the time. The cause had never been definitely established, but it was clear to him now that it was due to some of the anger and resentment he felt toward his wife. After his divorce, when he remarried, he had been frank with his new wife about most aspects of his first marriage, but his occasional bouts of impotence were something that he had hesitated to talk about. He worried from time to time that they might recur, and that he would "fail" her. As he became more open with his partner, Daryl decided he would feel more comfortable if he shared his fear with her. She responded with understanding, and they agreed that if the problem arose again they would talk about it right away and see what they could do about it together. He felt relieved that he was able to talk about this problem, and reported that his general enjoyment of sex had increased considerably as a result.

Things Your Partner Needs to Know

Are there things that you think it would be helpful for your mate to know about you—things that he or she might have wondered about but been afraid to ask, or might not even have suspected? If you want your loved one to know, tell him or her now.

Virginia had always pretended to have an orgasm because she felt David would be disappointed not only in her but in himself if he knew she only rarely had an orgasm when they were having intercourse. She was shocked to learn that a large number of women never had orgasms under these circumstances and that orgasms occurred more easily as a result of clitoral stimulation by a partner's hand or mouth. Since David was unaware of her needs, there really was no way in which he could learn to please her unless she was willing to discuss her past pretense with him so that they could begin to work on improving the situation together. Of course, this meant risking David's anger, but Virginia concluded that taking the risk was better than lying in a situation that was so intimate and important to their relationship.

What Turns You Off

Have you had experiences that make certain actions or situations turn you off sexually? If so, tell your partner about them. Discuss what you can do to avoid them.

Barbara, an attractive thirty-year-old woman, had enjoyed an active sex life before she met Paul. They had been living together for about six months, and although the relationship was a generally happy one, she found herself increasingly dissatisfied with their sex life. Paul seemed to be timid in the way he approached her—as if he were never quite sure whether he wanted to make love or not. If she initiated lovemaking, he went along willingly, but she resented that most of the initiation came from her and that he always wanted her to be on top when they made love.

He was also less experimental in his approach to sex; she liked more variety than he seemed to want.

Barbara had always surmised that her mother, a lively, fun-loving woman, had not been sexually satisfied because her father had been an invalid for many years. Although she knew Paul was a strong, healthy man, his lack of assertiveness in the bedroom made her wonder whether she would suffer the same fate as her mother. When they talked together, Paul revealed how limited his past sexual experience had been and how fearful he was that Barbara might leave him before he learned to feel more at ease with her "expertise." Living together was one way for this couple to find out if they could work things out sufficiently to enter a more permanent relationship.

What Turns You On

Are there particular practices you remember from the past which you would like to reestablish because they make you feel comfortable or turn you on? Tell your mate about them, and discuss how to restore them in your current love life.

Beverly had had a number of partners before she met John. One of them used to tie her hands to the bedposts and make love to her while she was helpless to move. There was never any real fear on her part that he would hurt her "but a little fear had been wildly exciting." She had even enjoyed being spanked by some men and she often wished John would try that. She hesitated to ask him for fear that he would think her perverted. When she finally did, at first John expressed his dislike of violence. Beverly suggested that they just talk about her being tied up as they were making love—"fantasize it together." John agreed and found himself excited. Gradually they moved into trying it out, with great mutual enjoyment. There was a definite agree-

ment between them of certain limits beyond which they
would not go.

Of course your partner may not always want to go along
with what you ask for. However, expressing your desires
helps your partner to examine his viewpoint, which in time
may change.

TURNING FROM THE PAST

By now we hope you've gained some perspective, so that
you are better able to understand why you have some of the
feelings and attitudes you have today about your sexuality,
about the way you relate to your partner, about your total
identity. This perspective can help you understand your
strengths, as well as some of the conflicts and negative feelings left over from your past. It may help reduce some of the
blame and anger you feel because things aren't just the way
you want them to be. You've also shared some of what you
and your partner learned about yourselves, so that hopefully
you understand each other a little bit more. Now put aside
the past and focus on what you can do in the here and now
to achieve the greater intimacy you're both striving for. Talk
about what you two have going for you: your love for each
other, your children, your jobs. Talk about what areas you'd
like to improve; how you can go about working toward
change.

At this point, if we were seeing a couple in therapy we
would introduce an exercise to encourage sexual communication. You and your partner can introduce this exercise
yourselves after you've worked on verbal communication of
your wants, needs, and expectations. Again, as in all the pre-

vious exercises, pick a time when you're relaxed and in a good mood.

EXERCISE: LEARNING TO LOVE

The purpose of this exercise is to develop a way to show each other what each one likes and needs and what feels good. It's a form of communication that avoids the criticism that we are all so sensitive to in the area of sexuality. To illustrate, we'll give instructions for this exercise to an imaginary couple, John and Ethel.

This session should start when you have at least two hours of relaxed, private time available. John, you might initiate this exercise and both of you should agree that the session will not end in intercourse. The purpose of this exercise is education, not sexual arousal. If either of you gets aroused and wants to go on to orgasm without coitus, that's fine, but don't feel that's essential.

You might begin again with a shower. When you get into bed, naked, and with the lights on if it's after dark, John, you sit on the bed with your back against the headboard or wall and your legs spread apart. Ethel, you sit on the bed between John's legs with your back against his chest, with your legs over his. We call this the toboggan position.

Many women like this position because it gives them a feeling of being sheltered and protected. Others enjoy it because as they instruct their partner in what they like, what they need, and what they want, they are not distracted by observing their partner's reaction. They can concentrate on their own sensations.

Some couples find this position somewhat awkward and uncomfortable because of their particular proportions. If it's like that for you, experiment with other positions until you find one that's right for the two of you. One suggestion might be for the woman to lie on her back and the male to kneel at her side, as in sensate focus (see pp. 64–68).

When you find yourself in a comfortable position, John, reach out with your arms and begin to explore and caress Ethel's face. With your fingertips trace her eyebrows, her eyelids, the shape of her nose, her lips; stroke her hair, play with her earlobes. Move down toward her neck, her chest, her breasts. Ethel, you guide John, put your hand over his and show him the pressure you like, the rhythm, the special places where you like to be touched. Remember that he can't read your mind. Teach him what it is you need and want. John, you focus in on what Ethel is communicating to you. No matter how good a lover you are, there is no way for you to learn how to give her pleasure unless she shows you from one time to another, from one moment to another.

When you reach Ethel's genitals, John, you might put a drop of Vaseline or KY Jelly on your fingertips, so that any irritation is avoided. If she's aroused by the touching and caressing, she might guide your fingers inside her vagina so you can moisten your fingers with her lubrication. Lubrication takes place on the walls of the vagina, and there is none on the outside. To guide John's stimulation of your clitoral area, Ethel, you might want to put one of your fingers on one of his; for the labia two of your fingers on two of his; and for the mons area, your whole hand on top of his hand. Show him if you like your clitoris stimulated directly (most women don't), or whether your prefer him to stimulate the area around it, the shaft of the clitoris or the labia.

If you feel the message isn't getting through, Ethel, put your hand directly on your body, and, John, you let your hand ride lightly over hers. That's another way to learn. If all this touching and exploring and showing makes you feel you want to have an orgasm, tell John to continue the stimulation. Remember, you don't have to show John what a good pupil he's been. If you don't want to go on to orgasm, stop when you feel like it and lie together for a few minutes, sharing your feelings, communicating what the experience has been like for you, whether the position was comfortable, what you've learned.

Then, John, you lie on your stomach and, Ethel, you get into a position that's comfortable for you to reach out and touch him: kneeling between his legs, sitting on the bed beside him or any position that works for you. Stroke and caress him as you did in the first exercise. John, if you can reach back with your hand, particularly around your buttocks and anus, guide Ethel's hand there. Then turn over and again let Ethel know what you like by guiding her hand. Place it on your chest, let her play with your nipples, move her hand to your abdomen and this time include your genitals. If you're using a body lotion be sure to use it on your penis, or use a lubricating jelly. Show her how you like your penis stroked, the rhythm, the pressure, the parts you like stimulated; some like the root and shaft of the penis to get special attention, some prefer the glans. Some like gentle touching, some like it firm. Some men like their testicles brushed up. Some like their thighs stimulated. Experiment and learn. If you feel like going on to an ejaculation, show Ethel how you bring yourself to a climax.

When we gave this exercise to Jim and Mary, Jim reported that he had found it highly arousing. He explained that he had always wanted to show Mary exactly how to stimulate him, but he had considered it too much to demand of her. By guiding her hand with a light touch, he had taught her all the "finer points" he used when he stimulated himself—"and I've been learning how for a long time." He had also enjoyed ejaculating outside of Mary's vagina, with her watching. "It's incredible that after all these years she really watched for the first time—with great curiosity." We agreed that a natural phenomenon like ejaculation is often never observed, but that it can be a really novel experience to watch, to touch, to taste, and to smell.

Mary, on the other hand, reacted with some disappointment to the experience because she had found it more difficult to teach Jim what she wanted him to do. "It was okay in some parts of my body, but sometimes his hand pulled away from my guiding hand, as if it wanted to go on its own." Jim agreed that he found it hard to know where Mary wanted to go—that he needed firmer guidance. It was suggested that one possibility was for Mary to put her hand directly on her own body with Jim's hand over hers. Also, Jim needed to concentrate on relaxing his hand.

Learning from each other like this is a way to truly communicate your sexual needs without words. As in learning any new language, it may take some time to convey what your preferences are and how they can be met, but it is time well spent. It may also make you aware that before you can show your partner what you like, you may have to learn a lot about your physiology, which we'll be discussing in later chapters.

SEX AS PLAY

The educational exercise described above is of great value and something you should go back to from time to time to become sensitive to each other's needs. But it is also a form of play, a way of varying the numerous ways in which you can make love. If you think of sex only as intercourse, it is bound to become monotonous and regarded as pressure. In reality, the possibilities of sex are infinite.

Try playing different roles. If you are normally passive, take a turn at being aggressive while your mate is passive. If you are normally aggressive, take a turn at being passive while your mate is aggressive. If you are normally nurturing, try being greedy for your own pleasure. Your sexual relationship can become an opportunity to explore and express all the various perceptions you have of yourselves. Learn to express yourself in words and in gestures.

Six

The Facts of Life

THE VELVET CURTAIN

Sex is an important dimension of every human life. Yet for the reasons discussed earlier, for most men and women securing reliable information about human sexuality has often been difficult. Sex has been hidden behind a velvet curtain of social and religious taboos which children, adults, and even scientific investigators have been forbidden to lift until recently.

The resulting sexual ignorance has been one of the most important barriers to sexual fulfillment. In the Victorian era it was not uncommon for marriages to remain unconsummated for years simply because the partners did not know how to go about having intercourse. In fact, we know of a contemporary case of a college-educated couple, the husband highly successful in business, who went to a doctor complaining of infertility. On examination, his wife turned out to be a virgin. They had for years engaged in intercrural intercourse (between the thighs) without being aware that conception could not occur without vaginal penetration.

While such extremes of ignorance are rare today, lesser misconceptions abound. If you are not well informed about the nature of sexual functioning, it can interfere with your sex life in a number of ways.

You may miss many of the pleasures of sex because you are unaware of them, or do not consider that they are normal and healthy. For example, many couples avoid forms of sex which involve contact between mouth and genitals. They might feel much more at ease with such activities if they knew that kissing the genitals is at least as sanitary as ordinary kissing, and that it is a common practice of many couples.

You may do things that interfere with full sexual response. For example, certain parts of the clitoris and penis are so sensitive that they can be painful if stimulated directly. Ignorance of this fact may make efforts at sexual stimulation a cause of exquisite pain.

You may feel guilty and ashamed unnecessarily because of ignorance of what is normal in sexual behavior. For example, Vivian felt there was something wrong with her because she had to stimulate herself during intercourse.

> I feel awful because I play with myself while Michael's inside of me. It's the only way I can come. Michael tells me he doesn't mind but I know he feels funny about it too.

Vivian was encouraged to read *The Hite Report*, a recent book by Shere Hite, which helped her realize that most women don't have orgasms during intercourse. Rather than agree with her that she should be ashamed of herself, we encouraged her to continue the practice. Many people harbor similar fears that some aspect of their sexuality is abnormal or perverse. Only by acquiring factual information about human sexuality can they dispel their fears.

CONTEMPORARY SEX RESEARCH

Fortunately, in recent years the velvet curtain of secrecy about sex has been lifted somewhat by serious scientific research into the nature of human sexuality. Accurate, reliable information on the range and frequency of various kinds of sexual behavior was first collected by Dr. Alfred Kinsey and his associates; other investigators have subsequently extended, updated, and generally confirmed his findings. The actual physiology of human sexual response has recently been studied in the pioneer laboratory work of Dr. William Masters and Virginia Johnson. Anthropologists have described the great range of sexual practices in various societies (and the different meanings attached to them). And much has been learned, both from human psychology and from studies of animal behavior, about the development of sexual feelings, relationships, and behavior in humans. This scientific knowledge is the firm foundation on which modern sex therapy—and sexual enrichment programs—rests.

We find that understanding the nature of sexual response in men and women and learning about the range of sexual behavior helps almost everyone feel more confident about sex, more relaxed about his or her sexuality, and better prepared to enjoy lovemaking. In the remainder of this chapter, we have tried to select from the vast findings of sex research the information we have found most helpful to couples in improving their sexual lives. We have also described some of the more common forms of sexual difficulty. If you find yourself feeling uncomfortable or "closing your ears" to some of this discussion, you can use that as a clue to reveal areas where you are uncomfortable about sexuality.

THE SEXUAL RESPONSE CYCLE

Our bodies have a number of physiological systems—the respiratory, the digestive, and the circulatory systems, for example—which perform certain functions necessary for individual and species survival. Your sexual and reproductive system is one of them.

Each of these systems has a basic physiological structure whose function is modified by individual experience. Virtually all of these systems had been carefully studied by science for many decades, but until recently the direct observation of the human sexual system in action was taboo. As a result, misinformation and misconceptions abounded, even among those presumed to be experts. Fortunately, the meticulous laboratory studies by Masters and Johnson allow us to describe accurately the basic pattern of human sexual response.

Just as the smell, taste, or thought of food starts a flow of digestive juices in your stomach and of saliva in your mouth, so various erotic stimuli automatically start you on the road to sexual arousal. The stimulus may be visual, such as seeing an arousing person or picture. It may be tactile, such as pressure or friction on the mouth, breast, genitals, or other sensitive areas. It may be purely mental, such as an erotic train of thought or fantasy. Whatever the stimulus, erotic arousal normally follows the same physiological patterns, which are remarkably similar in both men and women, unless for some reason sexual responsiveness has become inhibited.

With the beginning of sexual arousal, blood begins pouring into the sexual organs of the body and later muscles begin to contract. This engorgement and muscle tension transform the sexual parts of the body from their resting state into organs perfectly designed for sexual activity. If stimulation continues, these organs proceed through a sexual response cycle whose four phases Masters and Johnson have carefully chronicled. In addition to the sexual organs, the whole body is involved in the sexual response.

The Excitement Phase

The first sign of sexual arousal in a man is the erection of the penis. As blood flows into it, the penis enlarges and rises at an angle to the body. As arousal continues, the scrotum begins to rise and thicken, while the testes are pulled up into their sac. These are involuntary reactions; they cannot be willed.

The first sign of response to erotic stimulation in a woman is the appearance on the walls of the vagina of beads of moisture which merge to provide a smooth lubricating film.* A little later, the head, or glans, of the clitoris swells and the clitoral shaft increases in diameter. Engorgement later spreads to the outer and inner lips of the vagina, causing swelling and parting them somewhat. With continued stimulation, the inner two thirds of the vagina—an organ that at rest is collapsed like an empty sock—expands and balloons out. The lubrication of the vagina, the swelling of the clitoris, the swelling of the lips of the vagina—like the male erection —all appear to result from the massive inflow of blood to the genital region.

Engorgement also affects other areas of the body. In some men and many women the nipples fill with blood and become erect. Toward the end of the excitement phase, a woman's breasts increase in size. Either then or later, a rashlike "sex

---

* This moisture is not produced by any glands, as it was formerly supposed, but rather is vaginal "sweat."

flush" may appear on the skin of either sex.* Pulse and blood pressure rates begin to rise. In addition, the tension in many muscles begins to increase. The whole body and especially the sexual organs become far more responsive to erotic stimulation than in their resting states.

One common difficulty encountered in the excitement phase occurs when one partner becomes aroused more slowly than the other. We remember Ellen, who described herself as sexually unresponsive. She often didn't feel "sexy" when her husband approached her; she frequently wanted to say no, and sometimes did. Only when she wanted to please her husband more than herself did she go along with his persuasion. She noticed that on these occasions she usually ended up enjoying herself. It upset her, however, that she didn't get aroused as quickly as her mate, that it took her so long to get in the mood.

Actually, many people, both men and women, have to begin with touching and caressing in order to get into the mood for sex. Thinking sexually and fantasizing sexual episodes can also help start the process. In the excitement phase, many women are more easily distracted than men and need continuous stimulation. As Ellen discovered, "If I don't focus on my sensations, if I don't keep my mind on my body, I begin to think about things that have nothing to do with sex." Ellen saw this as a defect: "I'm not sexy enough." But to some degree everyone needs to tune in to what's happening in his or her body to avoid distraction.

Ellen was also concerned that her partner would get bored before she was "ready" for insertion. Women often need more time before they are ready and concern about this is common. A woman will frequently turn herself off, fearing her arousal

---

* Seventy-five percent of women develop this rash, but it occurs only in 25 percent of men.

will take too long. Ellen needed reassurance that she was entitled to all the time she needed, that her partner did not resent it, and that not worrying about it would help her become aroused more quickly. We also pointed out to her and her mate that lubrication in itself did not always mean she was ready for insertion of his penis. Finally, we suggested to them that she should decide when she was ready and guide the penis in at that time.

With advancing age, speed of arousal may decline somewhat. Consider the contrast between Harry, aged twenty-five, and Barry, twenty years older. Harry described himself as "easily turned on." The sight of his wife walking around the room was highly arousing to him. He liked to follow her around the room with his eyes, watching her as she prepared for bed, let down her hair, bent over to take off her shoes. He would usually get an erection "before I even get near her. I enjoy touching her—that's even more of a turn-on than when she does it to me. But what's best of all is to feel her getting excited—I can feel her nipples harden and she starts getting wet. When she just lies there, it is as if the wind goes out of my sails; I even lose my erection sometimes. It's as if the real excitement is in my mind, rather than my body."

Barry, at forty-five, worried because looking at his nude wife no longer produced an erection as it had done in the past. The fact is that most men over forty require tactile stimulation—touching, particularly genital touching. Visual stimulation is no longer as effective for sexual arousal.

The excitement phase may last anywhere from a few minutes to a few hours or even a whole day. Men may become erect and women lubricate repeatedly without entering the later stages of arousal. Or they may go on to the next stage, the plateau phase.

The Plateau Phase

In the plateau phase, the many changes of engorgement and muscle tension of the arousal phase become more exaggerated. There are several additional effects as well. In men the testes swell and rise even higher. In women, the outer third of the vagina swells, reducing its diameter by as much as 50 percent. This "orgasmic platform" assures a good fit and proper stimulation for the penis after penetration. The uterus becomes enlarged. The clitoris rises away from the vagina, shortens, and may become difficult to find.

When couples are unaware of this change in the clitoris, problems can result. Jim told us with embarrassment about his difficulty in "sticking with the clitoris." Edith would often complain that he seemed to lose contact with it as she grew more aroused. She implied that he was clumsy in this situation as he was in others. In addition to poor communication on the subject, both Jim and Edith were unfamiliar with the basic physiological fact that as sexual excitation intensifies in the female, the clitoris retracts. It disappears under the clitoral hood, which has become enlarged by filling with blood. Most women don't seem to enjoy direct stimulation of the clitoris at this point anyway, for it has grown too exquisitely sensitive. It is the stimulation around the clitoris, the rhythmic stimulation of the mons pubic area, or the shaft of the clitoris, or pressure against it by the male's pubic bone that usually seems to be most pleasurable. Although the penis does not directly touch the clitoris, the thrusting penis pulls on the labia minora (the thin inner lips of the vagina) and so provides clitoral stimulation via movements of the clitoral hood. Once both Jim and Edith became aware of this, they were able to focus more on what gave them pleasure and less on their conceptions (or in this case misconceptions) about the "right" way to do it.

The Orgasmic Phase

If sexual stimulation is intensified to a sufficient level, a reflex action known as orgasm is usually triggered. In both men and women this consists of a series of rhythmic contractions of muscles in the genital area, accompanied by the clenching of almost every muscle in the body and an experience of intense pleasure.

In women the onset of orgasm is heralded by an intensely felt spasm of the swollen outer third of the vagina—the orgasmic platform—followed by contractions of the orgasmic platform and uterus that occur every four-fifths of a second and then gradually taper off.

In men the orgasm has two phases. In the first, the organs and glands containing the elements of semen contract rhythmically, forcing their contents into the bulb at the base of the urethra. This is experienced as the intensely pleasurable onset of orgasm. In the second stage, the urethral bulb and the penis itself contract, starting at the same intervals of four-fifths of a second that marked the female orgasm and likewise tapering off. These contractions lead to the ejaculation of the semen from the tip of the penis.

Reaching orgasm can take a different length of time for different individuals. For many years the "simultaneous orgasm" was equated with optimal sexual experience in our culture, a concept that left many people feeling something was wrong when they didn't achieve it. Actually, different patterns have different advantages. Simultaneous orgasm has its own special value, if it happens spontaneously. But when orgasms occur at different times each partner can then savor the other's orgasm. Some couples prefer to have the woman climax first, allowing the possibility of additional orgasms for her. Many couples like to vary their pattern from one occasion to another.

The Resolution Phase

The orgasm releases the tension that has accumulated from erotic arousal and initiates the return of blood-engorged tissues to normal. The sex flush disappears, while pulse, blood pressure, and breathing gradually return to their usual levels. Thus begins the "resolution phase" of the response cycle.

In men the penis rapidly loses its erection after orgasm, then more gradually shrinks back to its normal size. Male orgasm is followed by a "refractory period," during which a man cannot usually be restimulated or have another erection. For a time the penis may be tender or even painful to the touch. The length of the refractory period varies from individual to individual and from a few minutes in adolescence to hours or even days for the elderly.

After female orgasm, the clitoris rapidly returns to its usual position and the orgasmic platform begins to relax. However, most women do not experience a refractory period. Many women, if restimulated soon after an orgasm, are capable of having additional orgasms without going through the resolution phase. Such a multiorgasmic capability is rare among men.

In the course of the resolution phase, the body gradually returns to its sexually unstimulated condition. In general, the resolution phase takes roughly as long as the excitement phase. It may take considerably longer for a woman who has not reached orgasm to return to a normal state. This is one reason why women like their partners to hold and fondle them after intercourse, rather than roll over and go to sleep. Another reason is that after lovemaking women seem to need some reassurance from their partner that they are still loved and accepted. It is as if they were saying, "I need to know that even though I showed you the sexual part of myself and let myself go, you still approve of me and won't abandon me."

That men don't seem to need this reassurance is probably related to their greater acceptance of the sexual side of their nature. However, if men have some difficulty functioning sexually, then they too need to be held and fondled, even though they may turn away to hide their humiliation.

THE VARIETIES OF SEXUAL EXPERIENCE

The four phases of sexual response describe a basic physiological pattern that is part of the biological makeup of nearly all human beings. But individual patterns of feeling and behavior based on this biological makeup differ enormously from person to person and from society to society.

Before the era of systematic research on sexual behavior, no one really knew very much about what people did or didn't do sexually. One of the important discoveries of research by Kinsey and others has been the great variety in sexual behavior. Some people never experience an orgasm, while others experience an orgasm frequently. One person may have no sexual partners in his or her lifetime, some only one, while others have many. Some individuals may be aroused only by members of their own sex, some only by members of the opposite sex, and some by both. Arousal may come from looking at pictures, reading, specific physical objects that have been given a sexual connotation, contact with animals, or a wide variety of fantasies. For some, arousal may last but a few seconds; for others it may continue for hours. Sexual activity may be limited to one fixed position, or it may involve contact between every conceivable part of two people's bodies, or the parts of more than two people's bodies. Sex may take place within almost any kind of relationship. And it may express almost any kind of feeling from indifference to hostility to love.

The variety of sexual behavior patterns found in different

cultures can be equally great. In some societies, for example, kissing and other oral contact is considered quite objectionable, while a delicate sniffing of each other's skin—unknown in the West and mislabeled "rubbing noses" by Western observers—plays much the same role as kissing in lovemaking. In some societies premarital chastity is rigidly enforced, while in others young people are encouraged to be sexually active. In some, masturbation is taboo, while in others the parents may rub their children's genitals as a means of soothing and comforting them. Some groups consider sex a solemn, even a religious matter; among some Eskimo groups, on the contrary, it is known as "laughing time." In Latin societies, sex is often seen as a realm of male dominance; among the Arapesh, in contrast, men are expected to be gentle and sex is seen as a relationship between equals. In some sexually repressive parts of Ireland, women almost never have orgasms; in other societies girls may learn to have orgasms before puberty and consider this experience a normal part of intercourse. The list of such variations could be extended almost indefinitely.

The significance of these variations is evident: there is no single correct mold that sex is intended to fit. Rather, sex comprises a broad range of practices which couples or individuals are free to sample, usually within the framework of the society they live in. Of course, this philosophy assumes that no one is hurt or injured during the sexual encounter, and that neither partner's sensibilities are violated. This is the basic attitude underlying our conception of sexual enrichment.

How Sexual Response Gets Blocked

We have emphasized that sexual response is a normal, natural physiological response, like digestion. Such processes can often be disrupted by an individual's life experiences. When you are emotionally depressed, for example, your appetite may dull; you may find that nothing tastes good and cease to eat properly. When you are under great stress, you may develop an upset stomach as excessive acids pour into your digestive system. If the stress is chronic, long-term digestive problems can develop, such as a stomach ulcer.

Probably no biological system is as easily disrupted by feelings and experiences as the sexual system. No matter how great their distress, people's bodies will sooner or later demand that they eat, sleep, breathe, eliminate, and carry out the other functions necessary for biological survival. Not so with sex. Its expression can be modified and disrupted. It can be denied and postponed indefinitely. The capacity to delay sexual response is useful: it makes possible a selection of appropriate situations and partners for sex. But excessive inhibition of the responses of the vulnerable sexual system can produce long-lasting and severe dysfunction.

FORMS OF SEXUAL BLOCKAGE

Given all the attitudes and experiences that are likely to interfere with natural sexual functioning, it should come as no surprise that Masters and Johnson have estimated that more than 50 percent of American couples suffer from sexual dysfunction at one time or another. These sexual difficulties may be mild or severe, but they are invariably distressing to the couples they affect. Fortunately, they can be greatly alleviated in a large proportion of cases.

We all bring to sex our own unique physiology and experience. For that reason, every sexual problem is unique. But there are a few specific areas in which most of these problems are centered.

Perhaps most common is the feeling that sex is just not as enjoyable as it should be. Instead of being a source of great satisfaction, it is a tense, unexciting, or even unpleasant experience. This may be true of early sexual experiences which don't live up to expectations, or it may develop within a long-term relationship when one or both partners seem to gradually lose interest in sex. A common result is that sex becomes less and less frequent, although there may also be a considerable difference in the frequency with which partners want to have sexual relations.

Another common problem is that sex becomes permeated with feelings of hostility and anger. Instead of being a realm of mutual pleasure, it becomes a struggle for power or a vehicle for expressing resentment.

For women, inability to reach orgasm is a common problem. Some women have never had an orgasm at all, sometimes because they have never had really effective stimulation. Far more common is the inability to have orgasms under particular circumstances, such as during intercourse or with a particular partner. These specific problems of women are dealt with in Chapter 9.

Many men experience difficulties with erections. Although such cases are rare, a man may never have had an erection firm enough to engage in intercourse. More common is a tendency for the erection to subside when a man fears that he will be unable to perform adequately, or when he experiences other anxieties. This problem may develop at any point in a man's life. It is discussed in Chapter 10. The other common male sexual problem is a tendency to ejaculate very quickly, which may mean before or just after intercourse begins. This means a loss of pleasure for the man and often intense frustration for his partner. Techniques for dealing with it are discussed in Chapter 10. Other men have difficulty in ejaculating at all, or may be able to do so outside of the vagina, or when they masturbate, but not during intercourse. Because this problem is difficult to treat, expert help should be sought.

PHYSICAL CAUSES

It has been our experience that most sexual dysfunctions are due to ignorance, faulty family and cultural conditioning, and myths, misconceptions, and anxiety about performance. However, a number of physical problems can directly or indirectly affect sexual functioning. An estimated 5 to 10 percent of sexual problems are the result of physical causes. For that reason, before beginning any sex therapy program, we give our patients a thorough physical and biochemical evaluation.

Good health and good sexual functioning go hand in hand. It is important to have a physical examination before you undertake any measures to improve or correct any sexual difficulties you are having. Your doctor may be helpful to you in many ways in answering your questions as well as in evaluating your general and sexual health.

It is particularly important to rule out physical problems through medical examination if:

• You have any concern about a physical condition.

• Either of you finds intercourse painful.

• The male is experiencing any difficulty with erections and has a family history of diabetes; or has been diagnosed as having diabetes.

• The male is no longer getting morning erections and/or is unable to get an erection during masturbation.

• You have any anxiety about a cardiac condition or hypertension which you feel may affect your sex life.

• You are experiencing difficulty in having intercourse or have never been able to effect penetration.

• You are taking drugs of any kind.

• You are dissatisfied with your contraceptive method or want to discuss contraception.

• You have not had a physical or gynecological examination for the past year.

Perhaps you have felt that your doctor was not responsive to your questions about your sexuality in the past. He may be freer to do so now, as opportunities have become available for doctors to learn more about recent research in the field of human sexuality. Medical schools now include courses in human sexuality and recognize sexual function and dysfunction as an important area of health care. Remember, initiating discussion of these matters is not only your doctor's responsibility, it is yours as well.

MEDICAL EXAMINATION

Make appointments for both you and your partner to be examined medically. You may wish to have this done by your personal or family physician, and gynecologist, or urologist, etc.

The purposes of these examinations are:

• To identify and treat any physical problem that might interfere with your sex life.

• To rule out any organic pathology.

• To allow you and your mate to learn more about your sexual anatomy and physiology.

• To give you an opportunity to ask questions and get accurate answers from your physician.

We suggest that, if at all possible, both partners be present for both examinations. This will allow both of you to become more familiar with your own and your partner's body. This joint physical examination will also encourage you to ask questions which you have been hesitant to raise. And if any physical problems do turn up, you will both be fully informed about them and therefore be able to communicate better about how to deal with them.

We suggest that before your appointments you make a list of the questions you would like to ask. Be sure to list any factors you think might contribute to your sexual difficulties, as well as any questions you may have about your own or your partner's sexual anatomy and physiology. Don't be ashamed to be curious about your own body and that of your partner.

Seven

Intimate Knowledge

It's Never Too Late to Learn

An important part of your sense of self is the image you have of your own body. Your body image determines the way you feel about yourself as a total human being. It affects the way you expect other people to react to you. It plays an important role in shaping the way you will behave in a variety of situations. This is true of your general body image, and of your image of your sexual anatomy and physiology in particular.

A knowledge of one's reproductive and sexual organs is very valuable in establishing a firm sense of masculinity or femininity, and the opportunity for acquiring this knowledge should begin in childhood. Unfortunately, in our culture, parents are usually not knowledgeable enough themselves to impart this information.

Getting to Know You

One of the best ways to become relaxed about any subject is to know and understand it intimately. Ignorance is not bliss in sex. In an adult relationship, there is no better way for both partners to acquire sexual knowledge than looking and touching. And there are no better live models for you to observe than your mate and yourself.

THE CONJOINT PHYSICAL EXAMINATION

When couples come to us, each partner is given a thorough physical examination, but in a very special way: each partner is examined in the presence of the other. This is done not only to rule out any physical problems but also to help them to learn about each other's bodies in a relaxed, professional environment. It also provides an opportunity for the examining physician to correct misinformation and dispel myths and misconceptions in the presence of both partners.

POLLUTION TABOOS

The taboo on women's knowing their own sexual anatomy seems to be particularly strong. In part this is because it takes an effort for a woman to see her genitals. But in addition, women have been admonished not to look, to touch, to feel, or even to know. As a result, many women have developed feelings of disgust and shame about their sexual anatomy. They often refer to that part of their body as "down there," a foreign territory they've never explored.

However, negative feelings are often associated with the genitals of both sexes. Some of the taboos and myths about sexual anatomy go back thousands of years to ancient pollution taboos. These pollution taboos often revolve around the fluids associated with sexual organs:

• Some people believe that semen is unsanitary (polluted). Women will sometimes describe a feeling of revulsion about touching or tasting semen. Even some men describe a similar disgust.

In fact, as we explain to our patients, "pure" semen has no bacteria.

• This can be said as well of the fluids which lubricate and protect the lining of the vagina.

• Among the most powerful taboos in many primitive societies and religious groups were those surrounding menstrual blood. Menstruating women were even isolated in separate huts. Food that they touched was considered unsafe to eat. The feeling that menstruation is somehow dangerous and unclean persists for many people today. In fact, menstrual blood is no different from other blood. There are no medical indications against having intercourse during menstruation, if it is aesthetically acceptable to both of you.

• No doubt part of the feeling of uncleanliness surrounding the genitals comes from the fact that sexual and urinary organs are close together, and in the case of the penis are identical. Children are taught that urine and feces are disgusting and dirty, and they attach these feelings to anything "down there." In actual fact, however, urine is normally sterile—far cleaner than saliva. Furthermore, there is no chance of a man passing urine during or immediately after ejaculation; a valve to the bladder seals off the erect penis and makes it an organ solely for the expulsion of semen.

GENITAL MYTHS

There are a number of other common myths about the genitals that interfere with sexual pleasure.

• Some men—and some women—feel that the vagina is a dangerous organ. They may think of it as having teeth, or being a bottomless pit. There is even a belief, common in locker-room folklore, that the vagina can sometimes "clamp down" on the penis and hold it captive. This myth has been attributed to the nineteenth-century physician, Dr. Oliver Wendell Holmes, Sr., who wrote a report, under a false name, purporting to describe such a case of "penis captivus." He later admitted the hoax, and no authenticated case has ever appeared in the medical literature.

• Another common concern among men is that their penis may not be large enough. Sometimes this worry develops in childhood, when boys often compare the size of their penis with their father's. Actually, penis size has no effect on sexual effectiveness. In any case, penises vary far less in length when they are erect than when flaccid; also, when erect, a smaller penis expands more than a large one. You can be confident that the size of your penis will not interfere with your capacity to give and receive sexual pleasure.

• Some men are afraid of injuring women by intercourse, and some women are afraid of being injured. Of course, if a woman is forced to have sex against her will, she can indeed be hurt. But the body of a woman who desires sex is admirably designed for intercourse. Her vaginal walls become covered with a lubricating fluid which facilitates penetration and thrusting. Her whole pelvic area, as it becomes engorged with blood, takes on a shape perfectly suited to accommodate the penis of the male. Her pelvic bones are padded with flesh that permits even vigorous clutching and squeezing. There is no reason that intercourse should lead to any discomfort beyond the normal muscle fatigue that often accompanies vigorous exercise.

Sex Is Natural

Many of the fears and myths about the male and female genitals are based on one central misconception: the idea that sex is an unnatural phenomenon, a part of human nature that is isolated and compartmentalized from other aspects of physical and emotional functioning and well-being. In truth the sexual response is a normal, natural physiological function, like breathing or sneezing. And, like breathing or sneezing, the sexual response is an autonomic, reflex action, natural and inborn. However, in order to elicit this response we have to learn modes of behavior that lead to it. We have to know how to stimulate ourselves, how to teach our partner techniques of stimulation, how to create the right mood and ambiance for this natural response to take over.

Exercise: Taking a Look

The purpose of this exercise is to get on intimate terms with your own and your partner's body, to acquire a better understanding of your respective anatomies and sexual responses, and to share your knowledge with each other.

A Woman's Territory

The male sexual organs are primarily outside the body and therefore quite easy to identify. This is less true of the female organs. We suggest, therefore, that the woman start by taking some time alone to explore the territory of her own sexual parts, for her own education and so that she can serve as her partner's guide. It is interesting to note that in some

African tribes, the genitals are called "the second face." We suggest you become familiar with your second face.

You will need a brightly lit room, a hand mirror, a firm space—such as the floor or a wide bed. You may want to start with a warm bath or shower. Tuck some pillows under your head so it is raised for comfort and for good vision. Flex your knees so that your feet are flat on the mattress, open your thighs so you can see better. You can either hold the mirror with one hand or prop it against something so that you can see the opening of your vagina in it. A cosmetic mirror with a flat base is good for this purpose. Adjust your position until you feel comfortable and you can see your genitals clearly. A small flashlight is often helpful to illuminate the area.

Your vagina is covered by the labia majora, or outer lips, which when not stimulated meet and serve as a protective barrier. Gently separate the lips and use a finger of each hand to hold them apart. Observe carefully what you can see inside them through the mirror. Touch the thin inner lips—the labia minora. See if they are more sensitive to stroking than the outer lips. In response to sexual stimulation, the labia minora become engorged with blood and increase considerably in size. This is followed by vivid color changes. If the stimulation is continued, orgasm almost inevitably follows these changes in color. You can see these changes if you use a mirror while you are stimulating yourself.

At the top of the inner lips is the clitoris, partially covered by a hood formed from the lips. It is unique in that it is the only organ in the human body exclusively for sexual pleasure. The penis has other functions in addition to affording pleasure, such as passing urine, or depositing semen for impregnation. Touch the clitoris with the tip of your finger; observe how exquisitely sensitive it is. You may have some concern about whether it is of "normal" size. It has been definitely established that there is no relation between clitoral size and its effectiveness in sexual arousal.

Between the clitoris and the vagina there is a small opening, the urethra, where urine leaves the body. The next opening is the vagina. Gently pull apart the inner lips and look at the opening. The vagina is a potential space: its two walls touch each other, but it can expand to accommodate a finger, a tampon, a penis, or an eight-pound baby. Slide your finger into the vagina. Rotate your finger inside. Touch the walls of the vagina. They are barely sensitive to touch and have irregular folds called rugae. After a woman has had her first child, the walls become smoother because the rugae flatten out.

Next, try to locate the most important muscle in the vagina, the pubococcygeus. Put your finger a couple of inches into your vagina. Now pull up with the muscle you use to shut off the flow of urine. See if you can feel it contract around your finger. (In Chapter 9 we'll give you some additional ways to identify this muscle, and to use it to increase your sexual pleasure.)

GUIDED TOUR

Now both of you are ready to explore each other's genitals together. This experience can be interesting, informative, and intimate if the bed is comfortable, the room is warm and well lit, and pillows and a hand mirror are available.

We suggest that you start by taking a bath or shower together. Put your hand on your partner's hand and guide it while your partner gently washes every part of your body, including your genitals. Dry each other off and get comfortable on the bed.

Every inch of your body can be a source of erotic pleasure. This is a good time for you to look at each other's bodies, stroke them, and discuss whatever feelings of shame or modesty you may have about looking and being looked at. (And it can be a chance to touch and caress each other all over, as described in the exercise in Chapter 3, but this is the time to emphasize looking.)

Try starting with the man's nipples. For many men they are a sexually sensitive area, which can provide considerable pleasure. During sexual arousal, they become erect like miniature versions of the female breast. The woman can try stroking them lightly to see if this occurs.

Now take a good look at the penis. If your partner has not been circumcised, pull back the foreskin so you can see the glans, or head, of the penis. At the tip is the opening through which semen is ejaculated. It is very sensitive to the touch, and can easily be irritated by too vigorous manipulation. Gently pulling on either side can open it up, showing the tube of the urethra within. Run your finger around the coronal ridge. Notice the track of the urethra from the tip of the penis through the shaft down to the root.

The woman can next take the scrotum in her hand. You will be able to feel the testes within it. One normally hangs a bit lower than the other, and one is normally a little larger. In the course of sexual arousal, the testes will rise suddenly toward the abdomen at the point when ejaculation has become inevitable.

Now it's time to take a look at the woman. Again, start with the breasts; they are rarely precisely identical. Touch the nipples and observe the small openings for milk to pass through. The nipples usually become erect during sexual arousal. Around the nipples are the areolae, the pigmented skin. They, too, swell with blood during arousal, sometimes so much that the erect nipple seems to disappear. The breasts themselves swell by as much as 35 percent at the peak of sexual arousal.

Now, setting yourself in the position you discovered comfortable when exploring yourself, pull apart the outer lips of your vagina, while your man holds or props the mirror so you can see the pubic area. Under your guidance, he should identify and gently touch the outer and inner lips, the clitoris, the urethral opening, and the mouth of the vagina. Tell him how it feels to have each place touched. He should gently insert one finger into the vagina, and see if he can feel the cervix, and if you use an IUD, the thread attached to it. If you have been able to identify the pubococcygeus muscle, try to squeeze it around his finger. He should bring his face close to your vagina so that he can see as much as possible. See what questions you can come up with for each other about your sexual parts, how they feel and how they work.

"FASCINATING"

"Fascinating" is the word we have heard men use most often to describe their reactions to their first close-up view of their loved one's genitals. One man, the father of four, said on viewing his wife's pelvic anatomy during our examination, "It's fascinating; I can't believe I never saw it before." He told us that for years he had read about the clitoris but had never really known where it was. "My wife used to ask me to come down hard on that area, but I never really knew why. I'm very much aware of what I learned in the examination. Seeing pictures is not the same as seeing the live model."

We remember another couple for whom the physical examination was of great importance. This couple who were in their early thirties, with two children, had been married for fourteen years. Their marriage was threatened because Andrea refused to have intercourse except on rare occasions. She never undressed in front of her husband, wore heavy, long-sleeved nightgowns to bed, and recently had taken to falling asleep fully dressed.

Andrea told us that her mother had described sex to her as something bestial and ugly. It was "something you'll have to do until you reach a certain age; then you won't have to." Although she was an elementary-school teacher, she knew little about sex beyond the fears her mother had implanted in her.

When the conjoint physical examination was described to her, she commented, "You must be kidding; I'm not that sophisticated." On the day for which it was scheduled she described herself as tense and said she had almost decided to call the whole thing off. But she also had a real desire to change; she went ahead with the examination, found it extremely interesting, and asked many questions about her body and that of her husband. "How could I have grown up and lived all these years knowing so little about my own body?" she wondered. Her husband stared at her pelvic anatomy and at one point exclaimed, "You know, it's really beautiful." Andrea kept repeating, "I can't believe this is really happening."

After the examination, she commented, "I feel easier now, less nervous. I learned about my own body. I never really understood it before; I wasn't even curious about it. I have covered it up even to myself for many years." It turned out to be a breakthrough in their sexual life. The next night she undressed in front of her husband for the first time in fourteen years—"after all, he's seen me already." And the night after she "undressed easier" and for the first time in their marriage, permitted her husband to touch her vagina. She was surprised to find that she was also able to look at his body without embarrassment. Most amazing, it turned out that she had been orgasmic all along, but had denied it even to herself. Breaking through the guard she had erected about allowing herself to enjoy her body was a big step toward acknowledging herself as a sexual person.

In the next three chapters we deal with aspects of sex that are more specific to men or to women. Nonetheless, our focus remains on both of you. Increasing sexual pleasure and improving sexual functioning for either of you means a better sex life for both. Developing new patterns of sexual behavior is far easier and more effective when it involves the cooperation of both partners. Even when, in the chapters that follow, we address your partner, you have a great deal to gain in your own individual and mutual sexual pleasure from the success each of you has with the exercises, and a great deal to contribute to that success. So we urge you to continue to go through these chapters together, and to share what you learn from them.

Eight

Men and the Pressure to Perform

THE "SPECTATOR ROLE"

Do you ever have the feeling that even in the midst of making love you are also observing yourself and evaluating your sexual performance? Do you ever find yourself paying less attention to your erotic thoughts and feelings than to whether you are performing the way you think you should? Masters and Johnson have aptly termed this attitude the spectator role. As one man described it:

> When we're making love, it's as if I am in bed with her, and yet at the same time part of me is standing in the corner, observing the part of me that's lying in bed, and saying, "Joe, I'm watching you; how are you going to do tonight? Are you going to get an erection this time, show her you can still make it, or are you going to reveal that you're losing your grip, that there's something wrong with you and you're not really enough of a man any more?"

Both men and women experience the spectator role at times. But it seems to be a particularly common experience among men who have sexual problems.

In this chapter, we will discuss some of its causes, the ways it affects your sex life and what you can do about it.

Why Men Become Onlookers at Their Own Lovemaking

Why do men fall into the spectator role? The reasons are deeply rooted in the way male sex roles are defined in our culture. Traditionally men are supposed to be achievers, to approach things practically, to strive toward ever higher goals. Many men feel that in sex, too, they have to reach a goal, to achieve, to score, to make it, as they are encouraged to do in the world of work and on the golf course. From an early age sex has been presented to them as a test of masculinity at which they must succeed.

Such an attitude puts men under a tremendous pressure to perform. The fear of failure looms very large. As a result it is difficult to abandon oneself to the pleasurable sensations and feelings that are necessary for sexual arousal and release. The man in the spectator role often feels he has a job to do, rather than a chance to enjoy himself. If lovemaking is more often work than play for you, if you find that you are often watching to see how well you're doing, it may help you to keep in mind the following points:

POTENCY IS NOT THE SUM TOTAL OF ONE'S IDENTITY. The penis is only a small part of a man's entire anatomy; its active sexual functioning is only a small part of his total life. But our male-oriented society—like many others—has made the behavior of the penis a symbol and focal point for a man's whole identity. Boys are taught from childhood that erections are proof of manhood; the greatest sign of inadequacy as a male is his inability to "get it up." This attitude, that the behavior of the penis is somehow an indicator of a man's worth and effectiveness, has been perpetuated by men and women alike; both tend to ridicule and belittle any man with signs of what they label, significantly, "impotence."

Bart, a broad-shouldered six-foot-three Texan, in his fifties, told us:

> I look like a man but I don't feel like one. When I'm with a woman and lose my erection I feel worthless—anything but a man. And the more I feel that way, the worse the problem gets—and the more impossible it is to get an erection.

Bart said that he got good morning erections and had no problem when he was masturbating. He had a very good relationship with a woman he had been seeing for about six months, but he hesitated to ask her to marry him because of his sexual problem. He explained that his wife had died of cancer of the ovaries about two years ago. Although they had had a good sex life over the years, it deteriorated rapidly during her illness. Weeks went by without any intercourse, not because she was unwilling but:

> I guess I was afraid of hurting her or maybe the whole situation got me down. Anyway, I think that was the start of my trouble. When I met someone I liked about six months later, we played around and I got a terrific erection, but I lost it as soon as I tried to enter. From then on, it's all been downhill. But now I've met Sally; I'm crazy about her, and if we can work this out, I'll be a happy man.

It is not unusual for a widower to have some difficulty in having an erection when he resumes sexual activity with a new partner. First of all, there is often the anxiety about being accepted all over again as a person and lover, which leads to pressure to perform in all aspects of the relationship. Often the courtship involves heavy meals and more alcohol than is customarily consumed. There is the expectation that one must have sex at the end of each date, rather than when one is in the mood. Often more significant is the pervading guilt that the partner is dead and the widower is alive, wanting to have a good time. There's the guilt left over from the period before death, especially where there's been a long and painful illness. Very often during the course of such an illness sexual interest was inhibited by the partner's physical deterioration, the fear of harming her in some way or even harming oneself through possible contamination. Although these fears are often groundless, they do operate strongly for many men. In fact, so common is this whole situation in affecting the widowed male's sexuality that it is referred to by therapists as the widower's syndrome. What helps to overcome some of the problems involved is to acknowledge some of the feelings that are operative. Bart had never expressed what he was feeling even to himself. Long talks with the therapist and eventually with Sally helped eliminate most of his guilt and he was able to recognize how normal and understandable his reactions were.

The next step was for Bart to become aware of how much pressure he was putting on himself to attempt intercourse every time he and Sally were together. When he was able to talk more openly to Sally, he realized that his assumption that she wanted sex each time they were together was false. They began to spend more relaxed time together without making intercourse the goal of each meeting. Eventually they shared an apartment, which meant that Bart did not feel he had to make love when he wasn't in the mood or felt tired after an evening out with Sally. The episodes of impotence decreased and Bart regained his confidence as a person and a lover. A few months after they moved in together, they sent us an announcement of their marriage.

Then there was John, who recalled his first episode of impotency. He was shocked, and the worst part was that his wife taunted him—"not very much, but it cut very deep. I felt too humiliated to say anything about it to her. But fortunately, things went all right for a while and I did get erections."

The second bout lasted longer.

> I feel it was related to her not enjoying it; I was concerned it was my fault. I began to sweat when I got into bed as if I felt I was on the line. Somehow I've never felt up to par sexually. I think it began when I was in high school and my penis didn't seem big enough compared to the other boys'. My wife had been married before; I used to wonder if she thought I wasn't as big as her first husband, but we never discussed it.

Opening up communication between partners is often the first step toward improving a problem of psychological impotence. Knowing how each one feels creates an atmosphere of greater understanding and support. Helping the partner to realize she plays some role is also important.

YOU CAN'T "WILL" AN ERECTION. Deeply entrenched in many of us is the idea that male sexual behavior is essentially a question of willpower. Men are expected to control their actions in many areas of life; indeed, in our competitive society this control is a prerequisite for success in business, sports, and other activities. Too many men carry over the same attitude into sex: they feel that if only a man has willpower, he can make money, build his company, win his tennis game—and have an erection any time he wants to.

The other side of this attitude is the inevitable fear that if you don't have full control of your sexual responses, if you do not have and maintain an erection every time you want to or think you should, you are somehow lacking—lacking in willpower, strength, and masculinity. Such attitudes condemn any man to being a spectator in his own bedroom, watching to see if he will prove his ability to "make it," or if he will reveal his inadequacy and "fail."

The most important fact of male sexuality, which these social attitudes ignore, is that no man can will an erection, any more than he can will his stomach to digest the food he has eaten. The reason is that erection, like digestion, is an involuntary reflex action, regulated by nerves which are not under the control of the will. An erection occurs when blood pours into the spongy tissues of the penis—and willpower is as useless in directing the flow of blood into the penis as in directing it into the head, feet, or any other part of the body.

Thus, in reality, it isn't willpower that is the key to good sexual functioning; quite the contrary, it is abandoning oneself to the ebb and flow of erotic thoughts, feelings, and sensations. This relaxation allows the sexual stimuli to get past the guard of the conscious mind and work directly on the nerves that control sexual response. That is why we advocate this philosophy: when you get into bed with your partner, you should simply wallow in the pleasure of the moment and go wherever it takes you. Leave your hopes for achievement and fears of failure at the bedroom door, and concentrate on *enjoying yourself*.

YOU AREN'T "OVER THE HILL." There is a widespread misconception in our society that male sexuality is something that isn't going to last forever. As men enter middle age, therefore, they are likely to scan their own sexual behavior for indications that they are "over the hill." At the same time, they may strive to prove by an exercise of willpower that they are still sexually effective—thereby cutting themselves off even more from the full experiencing of their erotic sensations.

The actual fact, as we shall see in Chapter 11, is that the sexual capacity of a healthy male can continue well into his seventies and eighties, with only a modest and gradual slowing down of sexual, as of other, physical responses. Ignorance of this fact leads men—and their partners—to tormenting and needless worry. We have known men who have stopped having sex entirely because they were convinced their sexual functioning was impaired because of aging. When sex therapy helped them resume their sexual life, they acted as if a miracle had occurred, rather than simply a return to what was a normal activity for men of their age.

Your Lovemaking Patterns

Another reason men worry about their sexual performance stems from the false assumption that every man is supposed to follow a prescribed sequence. If a man touches his partner, he feels obliged to get an erection. If he gets an erection he feels he has to insert his penis, and if he inserts he assumes that he must ejaculate. If he doesn't feel like going through this whole sequence of events, or is feeling anxious about his ability to do so, he may avoid even touching his partner. Such a man will often say, "I don't want to disappoint her. If I start touching her and I can't finish it, I'll feel terrible." Thus his assumption that every touch has to end in an act of intercourse turns out to sabotage the intimate contact so essential for a good sexual relationship.

The truth is that every man has his own sexual pattern and rhythm, and that it varies greatly from one occasion to another depending on mood, circumstances, and many other factors, such as fatigue. Most men have to be psychologically interested in sex before they can be aroused by touch. Most men find that they can be aroused only by manual or oral stimulation of their penis when it is already partly erect.

Give your partner a good explanation of how you do and don't get turned on, explaining your own personal sexual patterns. Show her how you masturbate, the rhythm and pressure you use, and let her bring you to ejaculation by hand if you both feel like it. Let her play with your penis, get on intimate terms with your patterns of response, touch the semen, taste it, smell it.

Just as every man has his own arousal patterns, he has his own erectile patterns, which vary from occasion to occasion. During one act of intercourse, for example, your penis may be quite flexible; on another occasion, it may be hard and rigid, while on a third it may alternate between the two. (Many women like this variation: some find that an excessively hard penis occasionally causes discomfort, while others may be unaware of any difference.) On one occasion you may go to bed with your partner, quickly become aroused, and proceed immediately to intercourse. On another occasion you may feel like lying affectionately with her, talking and touching, without an erection occurring. Another time you may have an excitement phase that lasts for hours; your erection rises, then subsides; an hour later you have another erection, which lasts for twenty minutes and then goes down; two hours later it happens again. Finally you go on to intercourse and ejaculation.

OCCASIONAL IMPOTENCE IS A NORMAL PHENOMENON

Since an erection cannot be willed, there are likely to be times when you think you would like to have an erection but it doesn't occur, or times when you lose an erection in the course of a sexual encounter. This is entirely normal. Unfortunately, neither men nor women are willing to accept this. Both you and your sexual partner are likely to be somewhat alarmed by it, perhaps even consider it a sign of impending impotence. Actually it is nothing of the kind, and if you don't panic you will find your subsequent sexual functioning unimpaired. Indeed, we often feel it would be beneficial for every man to have an occasional episode of impotence so that both he and his mate would learn that this is a natural, transient phenomenon that will not persist, and that is not worth a moment's worry. It is estimated that more than half of the adult male population have experienced some incidence of impotency some time in their lives.

How Erections Get Blocked

While erections cannot be willed, a number of factors can inhibit them. Here are some suggestions that you may find helpful in maintaining good sexual functioning.

DON'T GET TOO TIRED. If you are tired after a long day of physical or mental activity your sexual responsiveness is likely to be greatly reduced. Inadequate rest over an extended period of time can lead to a general state of fatigue with much the same result. As the saying goes, the spirit may be willing but the flesh is weak. A short vacation, getting caught up on your sleep, or just taking a nap before making love helps many men overcome an occasional bout of impotence.

DON'T OVERINDULGE IN ALCOHOL OR FOOD. Heavy drinking is a very frequent cause of impotence. As Shakespeare said, "It provokes the desire, but dulls the performance." On the other hand, a light drink or two, a glass of wine may heighten sexual desire and reduce anxiety or inhibitions for some people. A heavy meal, like excessive alcohol, acts as a sedative and should be avoided before engaging in sexual activity. Why not make a date with your partner before a meal—or, for those of you who are overweight, instead of a meal?

TRY TO REDUCE THE STRESS AND STRAIN IN YOUR LIFE. Acute or chronic stress is likely to interfere with the erection reflex. Depression tends similarly to reduce both desire and capacity for sex, just as it interferes with appetite and sleep. These conditions may well have a direct physiological basis through changes in your body's chemistry. Men going through periods of stress or depression—and their partners as well—need to understand that a decrease in sexual interest and responses is a natural, temporary accompaniment of both. If you are able to take this in stride, you will find that getting erections will probably not be a problem for you when the period of stress or depression is over. If you are under chronic stress or suffer from chronic depression, you may need some professional help to overcome your difficulties.

TAKE CARE OF YOUR HEALTH. Any disease which disrupts bodily functioning is likely to take its toll on sexual functioning, and a few, notably diabetes, can directly impair the erectile process. Fifty percent of men who have diabetes are impotent. Some thyroid conditions and other hormonal conditions (states of either deficiency or overactivity) can also affect sexual activity. A complete absence of erection under all circumstances and at all times indicates the likelihood of a physical problem, warranting a full medical investigation.

Some men may not achieve an erection when awake. However, if there is no physical impairment, they may get erections during sleep. This can be ascertained by studies made at a sleep laboratory. If the studies show nocturnal erections even though there are none while awake, the root of the difficulty can be presumed to be psychological rather than physical.

TALK TO YOUR DOCTOR ABOUT YOUR DIFFICULTY IN GETTING ERECTIONS. There are many reasons for doing so. First of all, sharing your problem is often the first step toward changing it. Your doctor may be able to determine by talking with you, examining you, and referring you for certain laboratory tests whether the problem has a physical basis. Whatever the causes are, he may be able to help you directly or refer you to someone else who is specially trained to deal with sexual problems. Even if there is no serious illness it should be obvious that good health habits can contribute to a better sex life. The current American interest in exercise, maintaining normal weight and eating a balanced diet will certainly help you to participate in and enjoy your love life.

CHECK YOUR MEDICINE CABINET. There are certain drugs that adversely affect sexual function. Most important are those that are taken to lower blood pressure, such as guanethidine (Ismelin); clonidine (Catapres); methyldopa (Aldomet); propanolol (Inderal); reserpine (Serpasil); spironolactone (Aldactone); and hydrochlorothiazide (HydroDiuril). Other drugs include those that are used to treat peptic ulcers; tranquilizers, such as Librium and Valium; and drugs of abuse such as alcohol, heroin, and methadone. (Librium and Valium can also be abused.) Obviously, you should not stop taking a drug prescribed by your physician without his permission. If you tell him about your problem, your doctor may recommend another drug in the same class that may have a lesser side effect.

IMPROVE YOUR COMMUNICATION WITH YOUR PARTNER. Try to share your feelings with your partner. Express your needs and wants and desires. Encourage her to express her needs and wants. You may find that she is more understanding of the problem than you thought and that she would like to be touched and caressed and feel close to you, rather than have you lie on the other side of the bed worrying.

THE "OFF SWITCH"

By far the most effective inhibitors of the erection reflex are anxiety and fear. The system which regulates male sexual arousal is extremely sensitive to what is perceived as danger. With the first twinge of fear or anxiety about performance the arteries of the penis become so constricted that the blood supply that would produce an erection shuts down, and the erection subsides. Since anxiety about sexual performance and fear of failure are so common among men in our society, it is not surprising that the off switch gets triggered very frequently. Thus these fears and anxieties can become a self-fulfilling prophecy; worrying can bring about the "failure" you were worried about. The off switch can also be triggered by overconcern about pleasing your partner. This results in distracting you from enjoying your own sensations.

THE VICIOUS CYCLE

A man who is thus worried about his sexual capacities constantly scans his sexual behavior for the signs of possible failure—just as the same man may scan for the first chest pain as a sign of oncoming heart disease. A few failures may destroy his self-confidence entirely and lead him to withdraw from sex as much as possible to avoid further humiliation.

Joan and Bob, a couple in their late forties, came to us for treatment of impotence and a complete absence of sexual contact. It turned out that they had had an enjoyable sex life until one night when they returned from a big wed-

ding where they had had a few too many drinks and attempted intercourse. For the first time in his life Bob
couldn't get an erection. Of course, it was nothing but the
pharmacological result of the alcohol level in his blood-
stream and considerable fatigue, but he didn't see it that
way. Instead he went into a panic. He made up his mind
that the next day he was going to perform "come hell or
high water." Simply because he felt under such great pressure, he was almost bound to fail. After two or three such
episodes, he became so disturbed that he could not even
touch Joan for six months. Finally, they sought help.

At the first session, Bob described his difficulty in getting
an erection as his problem: "It's all my fault." But he recognized that it created "misery" for both of them. The difficulty had been blown up out of all proportion and, as
Bob put it, "We just can't get together. She claims it's all because I don't love her any more. That's not the case. It's not
because of lack of interest that I don't approach her, it's
because of fear. Brigitte Bardot couldn't turn me on the
way I feel now."

Joan, a very attractive, vivacious young woman, told us
Bob had become very jealous. He was enraged if she even
looked at a man, although he had never been that way
before. Bob agreed; he was afraid she would leave him because of his sexual problem. He felt he wasn't the same person any more, in or out of bed. "I want to be the same guy
again and enjoy life. I don't want to be preoccupied with
this problem all the time. We used to have fun together;
now it seems we're fighting all the time."

Joan told us she had decided to go to work recently,
thinking it would ease some of the strain between them
for her to be out of the house, especially since their children were now starting high school. Bob had objected
strenuously, fearing her greater independence would increase the chances of her leaving him. "I can't help it. A
year ago I would have been proud of her working, now
I'm ashamed that I don't want her to."

Fortunately their problem—and most others like it—was not a reflection of any serious illness or psychopathology but simply a panic reaction based on sexual myths and misconceptions. Today, Bob does not feel he has a sexual problem. He still experiences occasions when he would like to have an erection and doesn't, but both he and Joan know enough now to pay little attention to it, secure in their knowledge that this is a transient condition that will pass. With the clearing up of their sexual difficulties, their other problems improved too. Bob no longer feels so jealous, and has been able to support Joan's return to work. The wall between them began to crumble and they started to have a good time together again. "Even my tennis game improved," Bob wrote to us, "because I've learned not to fall apart if my game is off for a few weeks."

YOUR PARTNER'S ROLE

Inevitably when a man is having difficulties with erections, it has an impact on his relationship with his mate. The initial reaction of most women is usually very sympathetic and supportive. They recognize that the situation can be very painful and humiliating for a man. However, the man may react inappropriately to her solicitude, taking her acknowledgment of the problem as a further humiliation. If the woman says, "You've been working so hard; maybe you should take a vacation," he may misinterpret it to mean, "She thinks I'm getting older and can't perform adequately any more." Thus he may reject her comforting, making her feel rejected and himself more miserable.

If the man becomes increasingly worried, locks himself even more into the spectator role, and as a result develops a continuing problem with erection, he is likely to start avoiding any physical contact. "I don't want the hassle, I couldn't be less interested," one man told us. As a result, his wife felt totally rejected, and it is this which is likely to genuinely disturb his relationship with his partner. As a woman whose husband had barely touched her in months complained to us:

> I don't really care so much whether we have intercourse; that's not what I'm mainly interested in. What I want is an indication that he cares for me. He hasn't touched me; he hasn't even looked at me; ever since he's had this problem he just rolls over on his side of the bed and I don't get any response from him at all. Sometimes I think that he doesn't care for me any more, that he's lost interest in me; maybe he's found somebody else.

WOMEN'S RESPONSES TO MALE IMPOTENCE

At this point a woman is likely to begin responding as much to her feelings of being rejected as to her partner's problems with erection. When he rolls over in bed and acts cold and disinterested, like Joan, she is likely to begin to wonder whether she has become unattractive to him, or even whether he has found somebody else. If she is feeling insecure about her attractiveness because she is growing older, his behavior is likely to worry her even more. So, feeling the problem is somehow a product of her inadequacy, she too withdraws. She remains on her side of the bed, he stays on his side of the bed, and neither one is able to reach out to the other with the kind of affection that might begin to reduce their anxiety and restore their sexual involvement.

This process rapidly erodes the communication between lovers. They don't talk about sex because they feel it is too threatening. They don't talk about the fact that they aren't touching each other. Soon they have trouble talking freely about anything. The man can't understand that his partner is withdrawing because she feels rejected; he assumes she is withdrawing because she considers him inadequate. So he can't reassure her about her fears that she may be growing old and undesirable. She in turn can't see that his coldness is really the result of his fear of failure, and that he is trying to close himself off not to her but to any situation that might be regarded as a sexual test.

Faced with continuing coldness, a woman who was originally sympathetic may eventually come to feel bitter and hostile. She may become sexually demanding. She may belittle her partner, and criticize his behavior in bed and out of bed. This is what was happening to Sylvia and Murray.

Sylvia, a sharp-tongued, critical person generally, began to get angry at Murray if he failed to have an erection. On one occasion when he had some difficulty she turned her back to him. Infuriated by her reaction, Murray decided to seek help. "What's wrong with him?" Sylvia asked. "He gets dead down there most of the time." Her anger only served to lower Murray's self-esteem and make him more anxious and concerned as to whether he could perform the next time they were in bed. It was as if they were trapped in a vicious cycle from which there was no escape, with each blaming the other.

The treatment we recommended for Sylvia and Murray included the exercise described below.

WHAT WOMEN CAN DO

As a woman you can do a great deal to help relieve the pressure for performance our society puts on men:

1. You can adopt the point of view that sex is not only intercourse but a broad panorama of experiences which may

or may not end up in intercourse, and enjoy the experience wherever it takes you.

2. You can take turns initiating sexual play and not expect initiation always to come from the man. This gives you an opportunity to respond to your own sexual rhythm and gives the man a chance to be the one pursued.

3. You can participate actively in love play, both for your own enjoyment and because of your recognition that most erections occur as a result of mutual excitation.

4. You should be aware that genital stimulation is of considerable importance in helping a man attain an erection. This is particularly true of men past forty, but frequently true of younger men as well.

5. You can accept more responsibility for your own sexuality, learn more about your needs, discuss sex more openly with your partner.

6. You need to accept the idea that less interest in sex at various periods of your relationship does not mean your marriage is threatened or that your partner no longer loves you. This may help you to put less pressure on your partner when he's not interested or has difficulty in getting aroused.

7. Finally, your immersion in your own sensual pleasure, and your encouragement to your man to do the same, is perhaps the best contribution you can make to transforming sex from a test or trial into an experience for mutual enjoyment. After all, an excited partner is the only true aphrodisiac.

FOCUSING ON YOURSELF

Focusing on oneself is particularly important for men because many of them tend to become preoccupied with how their performance affects their partner. Of course, concern about one's lover is one of the basics underlying a good sexual relationship. But that doesn't mean taking the "sentinel role," constantly watching to see whether you are getting your partner turned on, constantly worrying about whether you can make her come—in short, seeing her responses as one more test of your own sexual effectiveness. While it is important to focus some of your lovemaking attention on your partner's expressed needs and desires, it is equally important to learn how to temporarily tune out everything but your own pleasurable feelings and sensations, to immerse yourself in them, and to enjoy them to the hilt. Many men resist acting this way because they fear it is selfish. If that is so, it is a paradoxical selfishness, for the intense pleasure you thereby experience is likely to be as rewarding for your partner as any sexual attention you could pay her.

PERFORMANCE-FREE SESSIONS

For most men nothing can increase sexual pleasure so much as removing the pressure to perform. Every man needs to recognize squarely that an attempt to prove his sexual capacity is entirely self-defeating, because the best way to block an erection is to try to will it.

There is no better way to reduce the pressure to perform than by engaging in sexual activities which you have agreed in advance will not lead to intercourse, such as those described in the exercise in Chapter 2. Because you know you *won't* proceed to intercourse, because you have forbidden yourself anything that could conceivably be regarded as a test, you can immerse yourself completely in the pleasures of touching, tasting, exploring, and feeling.

We urge you to make such noncoital sessions a regular part of your sex life, to be tried once every few sessions. If in your regular lovemaking you find yourself playing the spectator role more often than you would like, watching your performance from a corner of your mind, try a few such "performance-free" sessions in a row; you may find you can give up the spectator role and develop a new awareness of the pleasures of sex.

EXERCISE: LEARNING THAT ERECTIONS CAN COME AND GO AND COME BACK AGAIN

Set aside a time when both of you are relaxed and in a good mood. It is best to arrange a session when you have no later plans, so there is no feeling of pressure because of lack of time. Agree beforehand that no matter how aroused you may become, you will not proceed to intercourse. This usually reduces performance anxiety and the fear of failure and creates a mood of anticipating pleasure, rather than achieving a goal.

This is what we told Sylvia and Murray:

> Sylvia, you might begin, as you've done before, stroking and caressing Murray with your hands, your lips and tongue. Use long or short gentle strokes, whatever you know from previous experiences that Murray enjoys; or you might place Murray's hand over yours to guide you. Move from one part of his body to another, from one erotic area to another, in a light, teasing, playful manner. Play with the shaft of his penis, the tip, his testicles. If Murray is not concerned about producing an erection, the chances are that he'll have one spontaneously. If an erection doesn't occur, don't despair or persist solely out of duty. Tomorrow is another day. If stimulating Murray ends in an erection, move your hands or mouth away and let the erection subside somewhat. Then you can start again, fondling and playing with him until there's another erection. This can be repeated several times.

When Murray and Sylvia tried this suggestion and he got a good erection, he told Sylvia, "With the trouble I've been having lately, how can I waste this one? Let's put it in." Sylvia reminded him that we had prohibited intercourse during this exercise. Murray rather reluctantly agreed.

Actually, the purpose of this suggestion is to take away the feeling of urgency that you must use every erection because who knows when you'll get another? The chances are if you have an erection and it subsides, you'll get another—if not at this particular session, then an hour later or the next day. It's a fear of not regaining the lost erection that is a big problem for many men. Actually, there is no reason for this fear since a man's erection, like a woman's lubrication, normally comes and goes several times during a period of sexual arousal.

If you want to have an ejaculation after several experiences of erect and subside, that's fine, but don't attempt intercourse until several erect and subside sessions have convinced you that even if you lose an erection it will return again:

When you do attempt intercourse, Murray, just lie on your back and relax. (Older men often have less difficulty in maintaining an erection with the man on top. Experiment with both positions.) Focus on your sensations, lose yourself in a fantasy if you wish, don't worry about pleasing Sylvia. Sylvia, you might straddle Murray, and play with him. If an erection does occur, slide down on his penis, guide it into your vagina with your hand. Move slowly up and down or side to side enjoying the sensation, without any vigorous thrusting. Then, slowly withdraw.

If either or both of you want to continue to orgasm outside of the vagina, fine. If not, hold each other and enjoy the close feeling that comes from pleasurable sensations without going any further. Another time, you may continue to ejaculation without withdrawing, if you feel like it.

This slow, gradual, nondemand approach to lovemaking is often very helpful in overcoming occasional problems with erection—even in instances where problems have persisted for some time because the fear of failure has become so deeply entrenched.

Is Impotence Increasing?

There are many reports that today more men are having difficulty in getting erections. Increasing social and economic pressures, the pursuit of unrealistic goals, the high divorce rate, are all cited as the reasons behind a possible increase in impotency. Even more emphasis is put on the anxiety many men have about their changing role in society and their perception of women as sexually demanding. The use of the pill and the IUD, it is claimed, convey a message that women are ready and available and it is up to the men to meet their sexual expectations.

There is no statistical evidence that impotence has increased. Throughout history there is documentation that anxiety about potency has always existed. What seems likely is that today men are more apt to seek help with problems in this area and to talk more freely to their partners about it. It may be that when women were not aware of their sexual rights, the problem was masked. It may also be true that the postponement of marriage to a later age and the increasing number of divorces may reflect some temporary difficulties for men. It has been proven that nothing contributes more to continued sexual activity than regular intercourse within a marriage.

Nine

Women and Letting Go

THE DENIAL OF WOMEN'S SEXUALITY

Sometimes the things we think of as most intimate, such as personal relationships and sex, are affected by social and historical influences of the broadest scope. Rarely has this been more pronounced than in our society's changing attitudes toward women's sexuality.

For much of history, a woman's role was to be subservient to the needs of her husband and children. This attitude permeated every aspect of life including sex. Sex was viewed as entirely for the benefit of the man; the woman's role was simply to submit to the sexual demands of her husband, to give him his "marriage rights." Any enjoyment she might receive was incidental; any discomfort she experienced was the price she paid for being a woman.

A large proportion of women regarded sex as a somewhat unpleasant chore at best, a painful humiliation offering only an unwanted pregnancy at worst. Most men wanted wives who were "pure," virginal at marriage and "untainted" by sexual passion. Female sexual pleasure and female orgasm were largely denied, and a woman who expressed strong sexual feelings was considered vulgar if not perverse. Nor did the medical profession of an earlier era offer any encouragement to the enhancement of women's pleasure in sex. The nineteenth-century physician J. Marion Sims, considered to be the father of gynecology, regarded intercourse as purely mechanical, a process whose sole purpose was conception. It was essential for the man to penetrate and achieve orgasm, but Dr. Sims considered the woman's experience irrelevant.

As women struggled to gain equal status with men in education, on the job, and in politics, it was inevitable that they began to think of themselves as having equal rights as sexual beings, too.

The Emergence of Women's Sexuality

Several forces have strengthened this new attitude toward women's sexuality. Scientific research has slowly but convincingly established the fact that women's sexual response is almost identical to that of men. Reliable means of contraception have greatly reduced anxiety about unwanted pregnancy, long one of the main causes of women's negative attitude toward sex. Last, and perhaps most important, women have increasingly refused to tolerate their subordinate position in society, as well as in a relationship, and men seem to be gradually coming to accept the justice of equality.

These changes have benefited women and men alike. Surveys over recent decades have found that each generation of women is more likely to enjoy their sexual activities, and more likely to have orgasms, than the generation before. Since, as we have pointed out, few things contribute more to sexual pleasure than an involved and excited partner, the result has undoubtedly been a better sex life for men as well.

SOME NEGATIVE SIDE EFFECTS

The new emphasis on women's sexuality, along with its positive effects, has created some problems too. The achievement of specific sexual goals is often valued above closeness, intimacy, and mutual concern. In addition, women have also become subject to what has been up to this time chiefly a male burden—the "pressure to perform." Just as a man may constantly watch himself to make sure he gets and keeps an erection, so a woman may observe herself to see whether she attains an orgasm. The spectator role is itself the very thing that keeps many women from relaxing and abandoning themselves to the pleasure of a sexual experience.

In reality, it is far more likely that a woman will have an orgasm by submerging herself in her own sensual pleasure. For just as a man cannot will an erection, a woman cannot will an orgasm. The purpose of this chapter is to allow women to explore a variety of sensual pleasures without any pressure to achieve orgasm. While the activities we suggest may in fact help you to become orgasmic, their immediate goal is to allow you to experience your own sexual feelings more intensely, whether or not they end in orgasm.

MISPLACED RESPONSIBILITY,
OR, I'M SORRY, DEAR

The new value placed on women's sexuality often puts inappropriate pressure on men as well. With the increased importance of sex in their lives, women need to take far greater responsibility for their own sexuality, their needs, their wishes and desires. Unfortunately, this is not always recognized. Instead, the new sexual value system often places responsibility for a woman's sexual fulfillment on her partner. It is assumed that it is his job to see that she is properly stimulated so that she becomes aroused and reaches orgasm. The result is that for many couples, whether a woman reaches orgasm becomes a test for the man, as well as for her. If she doesn't, her lover feels there must be something wrong with *him*, with his technique or masculinity, because he couldn't "make her come." He is also likely to feel guilty: he knows he is supposed to give her this pleasure, but he hasn't. The result of his feelings of guilt and inadequacy, and the increased striving they may call forth, may well be to reduce his own pleasure and involvement in lovemaking, and lead him to an increasingly detached and mechanical approach, or even create difficulties in his functioning.

A man's preoccupation with making his mate reach orgasm is usually well meant, but it places her in a difficult position. She is bound to experience it as pressure—at a moment that she should feel free to let go and allow nature to take its course. In addition to whatever disappointment she herself may feel about not reaching orgasm, she now has to feel guilty about disappointing her partner as well.

Such disappointments can easily be transformed into hostility. A woman may blame her mate for not "giving" her sexual satisfaction. He in turn may interpret her lack of response, even to his strenuous efforts to arouse her, as a deliberate coldness toward him; and indeed, women sometimes will block their own sexual responsiveness as a way to express hostility toward a mate. In any case, she is likely to be turned off by his increasingly mechanical approach, and complain that his lovemaking lacks feeling for her. To be attacked while he is trying so hard is likely to leave the man feeling, "What's the use?" so that he eventually gives up what has become a struggle to satisfy his partner. She may interpret this as a rejection of her, or a further sign of selfishness on his part. Eventually the couple may end up frozen into rigid postures of mutual resentment.

This is just what happened to Charles and Phyllis, a couple in their early thirties whose marriage was deteriorating rapidly. They had fallen in love and married in their late teens. Neither of them had had much sexual experience before marriage, but they both somehow assumed that it was Charles's responsibility to induct Phyllis into the joys of sex. In the beginning, Phyllis told us, "It certainly didn't measure up to what I had anticipated. But I was very much in love with Charles, and I had confidence that things would work out."

As time went on, Charles was feeling more and more unhappy about Phyllis's obvious lack of enjoyment. He didn't talk with her about it, however; he felt it would hurt her feelings and besides, he blamed himself. "I knew I must be doing something wrong." He went out and bought a collection of sex manuals. They all emphasized the importance of adequate clitoral stimulation of the female, and he was convinced that that was where he had failed.

By this time Phyllis was beginning to wonder whether there might be something wrong with her. "I felt incomplete—not a whole person." The women at work discussed sex over lunch and she knew that she wasn't having the kind of feelings they described. The earth didn't turn, bells didn't ring. When Charles began making what she interpreted as desperate efforts to make her come, she felt a sudden pang of anxiety—realizing for the first time that their sex life was making him unhappy. She knew it wasn't a solution, but she began to avoid sex when she could, making excuses that she was too tired, had a headache, or just didn't feel like it. It was better than what happened when they made love.

As Charles tried harder and harder to stimulate her when they did have sex, Phyllis began to resent his efforts. For one thing, he was not very gentle. She tried to hide her winces, but with less and less success. For another thing, she found herself completely turned off by what she thought was the cold, mechanical way Charles tried to stimulate her: "It's as if he weren't enjoying what he was doing; it was as if he were doing a job."

And that's exactly how Charles felt; it was too much of a hassle to keep on trying. One day he began to talk to Phyllis about his feeling that something had to change; he couldn't go on this way. Their opening up to each other about the problem was a constructive step toward eventual improvement in their sex life. What came out of their first hesitant revelations to each other was that Phyllis relied so heavily on Charles to give her pleasure because she was so ignorant of her own needs. She had never masturbated, never even fully explored herself. She was sure Charles would be upset if she began to tell him what to do. Charles disagreed, saying he would welcome it since from his point of view he had tried everything. He promised to give her every encouragement in her attempt to learn more about herself. She was surprised to hear that Charles masturbated frequently and saw no reason why it was "for men only." Phyllis and Charles worked hard to learn more about themselves and each other, and to be open about their needs. Eventually they worked out a more satisfactory relationship.

SOME THINGS THAT WOMEN WANT

For many women, asking for what they need and want is still difficult, because it is in such sharp contrast to the way they were reared. In the past, being assertive sexually was interpreted as being aggressive, oversexed, unfeminine. To indicate that your lover was less than perfect was an insult to his sensitive masculine ego. Perhaps you still feel this way, or you may feel there is something wrong with what you want or wrong with you for requesting it. You may feel that no man can be expected to have the patience to caress you for as long as you require to become aroused.

Perhaps you want more variety in your lovemaking or more fun. One way to achieve those goals is to talk them over with your partner. We suggest that you discuss the following items with your mate, and identify those you think might make a difference for you. This discussion is an opportunity for him to stop guessing and really find out what you would like.

• Would you like to spend some time talking together and enjoying each other's company before making love? This is part of the "warmup" that many women need to become sexually aroused. Explain to your partner that he can't expect to sit reading the paper or watching TV and find you in the mood for love "on demand." You might suggest having a relaxed, loving time together, no matter how short, before getting into bed together.

• Would you like to spend a little longer in foreplay? Tell him so. It takes most women longer than men to become aroused and they need more time before they are ready for penetration. Show him the kinds of things you would like. And take the initiative in pleasuring him before intercourse, too, so that it becomes a matter of mutual enjoyment. A good rule for many couples is for the man to wait for the woman to insert the penis when *she* is ready. Remember, lubrication alone is not a sign of readiness, but expansion of the vagina is.

• Would you like to have your orgasm first, before, or instead of intercourse some of the time? Do you feel free to stimulate yourself when you want to? Or to ask your partner to stimulate you? Would you like to have lovemaking sessions that sometimes consist only of touching, holding, and caressing?

• Would you like intercourse to continue for a longer time before he ejaculates? Many women feel that their lovers ejaculate too soon because they are selfish and care only about their own satisfaction, and that their own sexual frustrations are the result of their partner's ejaculating too quickly. Many men do in fact reach ejaculation quite rapidly, leaving their partners unsatisfied. This is usually not the result of selfishness, however, but of not knowing the proper way of lasting longer. Fortunately, almost all men can learn to last longer by using the simple techniques presented in Chapter 10. We urge you to read this chapter together and try its approach. One word of caution is in order, however: many women don't have orgasms during intercourse, no matter how long penetration lasts. While couples who would like to extend their lovemaking should certainly try the method in Chapter 10, don't be disappointed if longer intercourse doesn't guarantee an orgasm for the woman. And by the same token, don't assume that the blame for any sexual frustration you may feel necessarily lies with your mate's rapid ejaculation. This assumption can be one more expression of the myth that it is the man's obligation to know how to arouse his partner. While he certainly should do the things you tell him will help, you need to know what you can do to increase your own sexual pleasure. Later in this chapter we will make some suggestions about this.

• Would you like him to take more initiative sexually? Tell him what would turn you on. If you would like him to interrupt you in whatever you are doing and try to seduce you when he's feeling lustful, tell him so. Find out if there is anything in the way you respond to his advances that makes him wary of taking the initiative.

• Would you like him to be less demanding sexually? Tell him you would prefer that he invite you to make love, rather than just assuming you will be available whenever he wants you. But be sure to reply with enthusiasm when he invites you and you do feel like having a sexual encounter. At the same time, make a point of inviting *him* to make love when *you* feel like it.

• Would you like more opportunity to take the initiative? The chances are your partner would welcome it.

• Would you like him to spend more time holding and caressing you in the afterglow of lovemaking? Women seem to need this more than men. Explain that only a few extra moments means a lot to you.

• Would you like him to be less preoccupied with work and more attentive to you? Find out what kinds of pressures he is under on the job and what would help him leave them behind when he comes home. In some families a cocktail and a conversation before dinner help mark the end of the working day and set the mood for a warmer and more relaxed way of relating. Others use a swim or a game of tennis to get their minds off their work. Some people need a cooling-off period by themselves before they can relate to their partner. See if you can develop techniques that can serve as a "decompression chamber" for dissipating the pressures of work for both of you.

• Would you like him to share more interests with you? Discuss the areas of mutual interest you have shared in the past and think about how you can expand them. We find many couples who started out with strong common interests which have gradually faded from their lives. Whatever you enjoy in common—a sport, a craft, reading about a favorite subject, or any other activity—discuss how you can spend more time together doing it.

• Would you like him to help you more with household responsibilities and child care? Maybe you feel he should help more without your having to ask him. That would be nice, but it's better to ask than to build up resentment; maybe he doesn't know what you'd like him to do or he needs some reassurance that the help he offers does ease your burden. Sexual life is very much affected by your feelings outside the bedroom.

• Would you like him to be more interested in your job or career? Perhaps you feel he resents your outside life. Talk this over together; maybe each of you needs to make some changes in your life-style.

There may be particular signs and gestures of affection that mean a great deal to you, but which you don't receive from your mate. You may miss not getting a greeting kiss when you and your loved one have been apart. Many women complain, "He never tells me he loves me." Such things may have great importance for you which your partner is not really aware of, for such signs of love are usually rooted in the ways we saw our own parents express affection to each other and to us. They are also closely connected with the different ways boys and girls are reared. As a result, men and women often differ on the terms under which they have sex. It's as if they each had a different script, which they rarely discuss with each other. The script may go something like this: He wants to make love; he feels aroused by sexual stimuli he's been reacting to all day. Or you may feel he's only responding to a biological urge: he's been watching TV all night and practically ignoring you. Or if he's been sullen all evening because you forgot to pick up his suit at the cleaner's, you can't understand his wanting to make love, and you certainly don't want to unless he woos you first. Explain to your man that the mood is important to you, and how its absence makes you feel. Keep in mind that his approach is not necessarily insensitive; he may march to a different drummer. Perhaps with some discussion he will appreciate your point of view and try to make some changes. But don't start off the discussion by saying, "You don't pay attention to me," or "You'd rather watch football than listen to me, so don't expect me to be interested in sex." Instead say, "It would mean a lot to me if we spent some time together before going to bed."

A Woman's Responsibility

You may agree on your need to broaden your sexual horizons, but by now you may also be wondering how you are supposed to do so. The rest of this chapter is designed to outline a series of practical steps you can take to increase your sexual awareness, deepen your sensual pleasure, and let you and your mate share in exploring ways you can give each other pleasure. Your willingness to get in touch with your own needs and capacities and to teach your partner about them is just what we have in mind when we talk about women taking responsibility for their own sexuality.

A Man's Support

Just as every woman should seek to become familiar with her erotic needs, her man should make every effort to support and encourage her. The more knowledge she has of her own sexuality, the more pleasure she will be able to get in her relationship with her partner. The more she feels responsible for her own sexuality, the less pressured her man will feel to perform. If she can tell him what she wants and needs, he won't have to try to read her mind, and will be able to relax and pursue mutual pleasure. If they are aware of these possible consequences, men should be pleased by women's interest in exploring and expressing their own sexuality, and should communicate their approval. A man's support can play an important part in encouraging a woman's sexual development.

Another way men can cooperate is to encourage their partners to show them what they would like. Although a woman needs to take the initiative in telling her man what she needs and wants, she usually feels very vulnerable, and wants to feel reassured that this is acceptable. Men should not regard women's suggestions as criticisms and should affirm that they want to please their mates. If a man is sensitive to his lover's suggestions, as many men are, it's a good idea to use the nonverbal exchange we've described in Chapter 2. If verbal discussion seems called for, try to talk together outside the bedroom, while you're taking a walk or a drive.

A MAN'S UNDERSTANDING

At times, a man may find it difficult to understand his wife's unwillingness to indulge in certain sexual practices, such as oral-genital play. Although this is a form of sexual activity widely practiced by many couples, some women are resistant to such activity because of their background or moral principles. If you feel resentful because your partner finds some practices unacceptable, understanding her position will be much more likely to produce change than making her feel guilty about depriving you of something you want. Forcing or demanding something of another person often lays the groundwork for anger and resentment. Respecting your partner's right to make her own decision as to what is or is not acceptable makes lovemaking enjoyable, no matter what is included or left out. The same principles apply if the man is the reluctant partner.

Don't generalize when discussing new practices that one of you would like and the other opposes. It's unlikely that telling your partner, "You're sick," or "You're perverted," will change anything. It would be better to say instead, "I know you'd like oral sex, but I feel somewhat uncomfortable about it. I guess the old prohibitions still hang on. Let's not do it right now," or, "I'd like to have oral sex with you. Maybe we can try it once or twice and if you still feel unwilling, I can respect your feelings." In this approach resentment is avoided and understanding is enhanced.

NEGATIVE CONDITIONING

Virtually every woman in reasonably good health has the physical capacity to enjoy most aspects of the broad panorama of sex. But negative conditioning toward sex and the fear of losing control greatly interfere with that capacity. For example, touching and being touched is for most people a genuine pleasure. However, these experiences can be uncomfortable and even painful to a woman who feels tense and whose muscles are clenched. Such tension may result from the anxiety she learned to feel over the years about sex in general. It may result from anger or poor communication and a lack of trust in her partner. It may be an inability to seek trust and acceptance in any relationship. Or it may be the result of traumatic experiences—rape, incest, unhappy sexual relationships—in her past.

As we have seen, most women from an early age receive an antisexual education. They are taught to conceal and repress their sexual thoughts, feelings, and impulses. They learn to hide anything that might reveal them to be too interested in or desirous of sex. Talking about sex is generally less acceptable in girls than in boys. Fewer young girls than boys masturbate. As one woman described her sexual education to us, "There wasn't a single 'do'; it was all 'don'ts.'" There certainly have been changes in the sexual climate but most people, even those in their twenties and thirties, received their early sexual indoctrination when attitudes toward sex were still almost exclusively restrictive and negative for women.

A negative attitude toward sex often reflects a negative attitude toward other areas of one's functioning. If you don't feel good about your sexual self, you probably don't think you're smart enough, or good enough, or worthy of someone's admiration. Your self-esteem plays a big part in your ability to let go and abandon yourself to the pleasure of the moment. Improving your sex life means trying to build your self-esteem in other areas of your life.

LETTING GO

A common theme echoed by young women is, "I get aroused to a certain point, but then I can't seem to let myself go." Often they will describe a fear of losing control.

The starting point for this inhibition is often early training in concealing and controlling sexual feelings, but it seems to have other roots as well. Many women worry about what their partners will think of them if they act in an uncontrolled and potentially "wild" fashion. They fear their partner will consider them oversexed, or find them threatening, wanton, or perverse. Many women are themselves afraid of what will happen if they lose conscious control of their actions, and instead are controlled by the involuntary reflex actions which occur in sex. They feel like the woman who told us, "I'm afraid I'll explode and the pieces will fly in all directions." Or the one who said, "I'm afraid if I start enjoying sex too much, I'll lose control and become promiscuous." Or "I'm afraid it will change my whole life."

Some women find it helpful to try role-playing the loss of control. Take your clothes off, lie down in bed, and act out the most outrageous loss of control you can imagine. In the throes of the most extreme sexual abandon—yell, scream, thrash about, and do whatever other "terrible" things you might feel wary of. You can try it first by yourself, then, if you wish, with your partner. It doesn't work for everyone, but it does help some women feel more comfortable about letting go. Watching yourself in a mirror as you pretend to have an orgasm is another way to help see the humorous side of letting go.

EXERCISE: SENSUAL EXPLORATION

Sensual exploration is an exercise designed to allow women to explore and get in touch with their own sensual feelings in a context that is completely under their own control. Plan to spend an hour or so of relaxed, undisturbed time alone.

This is an opportunity to be completely self-centered in exploring your own pleasure. Start by taking a shower or a good long soak in the tub, to relax your body. Pat yourself dry and get out your favorite body lotion. Be sure the room is pleasantly warm, and warm the lotion before using it.

Give yourself permission to enjoy the feel of your body as you apply the lotion.

Look at yourself in the mirror as you give yourself a slow rubdown. Start with the top of your head and work down the front of your body, including your breasts and genitals, to your toes. Take your time, and spend a minute or two on each part. Since you can control the touch exactly, you will be able to make sure that it feels good. Focus on the good feelings.

With your eyes closed let your imagination roam. What physical sensations give you pleasure? Go back as early as you can remember in your childhood. Can you remember the feel of sitting on a grown-up's lap? Do you have memories of running barefoot in the woods or on the beach? Do you remember the feel of a warm bath or a tingling shower? Can you remember the velvety feeling of your pet cat or the furry coat of your favorite dog?

Think about the *sensual* experiences you enjoy in the present. Do you like to swim, or to feel the surf against your body? Do you like to lie in the sun and feel its rays penetrate your skin? Do you like the feeling of satisfying fullness after a good meal? Do you like to cuddle? See how many sensual experiences you can think of that you enjoy, and let yourself imagine how they feel. Tune in to how your body feels as your mind explores pleasant thoughts.

Now, try to recall some sexual experiences in the past that have been pleasurable—a romantic setting, an erotic experience, a playful encounter you've enjoyed. Give yourself permission to think and feel sexual and to give yourself pleasure. If you want to learn how to have an orgasm, you need to feel relaxed and give yourself reassurance that what you're doing is normal and healthy.

Learning to Have Orgasms

If you are in good health, you can learn to have orgasms. But that doesn't mean that you can have them under any and all conditions. Women who have never had an orgasm can often learn to by reading a book, or joining a women's group, or working with an individual therapist. In time, they can transmit what they have learned to their partner. It's much more difficult to learn how to have an orgasm during intercourse, and it is estimated that only 30 to 50 percent of women have orgasms in that way. Even though women may know this intellectually, they often consider themselves inadequate sexually if they don't reach orgasm during intercourse. Sometimes their male partner considers them frigid if they don't climax in this way, or he may consider himself an inferior lover. We feel that an orgasm is an orgasm, whether it occurs during or outside of intercourse.

Teaching yourself to have orgasms involves finding the time to discover the conditions under which you can have them, and trying to create those conditions when you want to have an orgasm. If you are like many women, however, you probably feel some reluctance to take this step. For a long time there has been a taboo on women's masturbation. Genital exploration is a natural activity which most little girls try, but for which they are often punished if caught. Adolescent masturbation is perhaps the most natural way for young women to develop their capacity for orgasmic response, but for many it is still enveloped in shame and guilt. Many adult women masturbate only furtively, and feel there must be something wrong with them for doing it.

This is unfortunate for several reasons. According to Kinsey's studies, women who masturbate in their youth are considerably more orgasmic in their mature sex life than those who don't; indeed, adolescent masturbation may be the best preparation there is for a good sex life. Masturbation allows women a sexual response that is completely under their own control. Therefore, it is a way to learn that you need not worry about "losing control" or "letting go" during sexual arousal. Finally, masturbation is in its own right a normal and natural means of achieving sexual pleasure and relieving sexual frustration when your mate is absent, ill, or otherwise not available for sex, or if you are without a partner for a period of time.

EXERCISE: SEXUAL EXPLORATION

The purpose of this exercise is to provide an opportunity to learn about the responses of your own body. Just try one step at a time, and repeat each step until you can do it easily and enjoyably before proceeding to the next. This exercise should be particularly valuable for you if you have difficulty reaching orgasm, or you've never had an orgasm.

At a time when you can have uninterrupted privacy for a few hours, start with a shower or bath and lie down on a comfortable surface—your bed or a rug on the floor. (You may want to have a little lubricant jelly at hand to use if you feel like it.) Try to spend a few minutes enjoying whatever sensual experiences you found pleasurable in the previous exercise. Lie on your back with your legs spread and your knees bent, and begin to explore all the parts of your genitals with your hand. Use a hand mirror so you can see what you are doing. Try touching your outer and inner lips, the opening of your vagina, the hood and shaft of your clitoris, and all the areas surrounding them, particularly the mons veneris, the hairy pad above the vulva. Take your time, don't concentrate on any particular area, but explore in a leisurely way your whole genital region. Take note of any areas that are particularly pleasurable or stimulating to your touch.

Now try focusing your attention on the pleasure-creating areas you have found. Experiment with different rhythms, pressures, and moistures—such as a lubricant jelly, some unscented oil, or your own saliva. Try deep rubbing and friction on the surface. Find out what kinds of stimulation you find sexually arousing.

Now see how much you can increase the intensity of your sensations. If an orgasm occurs, fine. If it doesn't, keep going until you get tired or feel sore. Some women when they are first learning may take from forty-five minutes to an hour of intense stimulation before they reach orgasm. If you find yourself growing bored, or your mind wanders, try to refocus yourself with a fantasy.

Some women get discouraged if they do not reach a climax after many sessions of intense and continuous stimulation. They tell us there must be something wrong with them—"I'm frigid," as one woman put it; "maybe my wiring is defective." If you're discouraged after using your hands without success, it would be a good idea to buy an electric vibrator and see if the extra stimulation it provides works for you. If it does, it will convince you that you are capable of a normal, healthy sexual response. It will also give you a mental and physical model of what an orgasm is like, so that you can strive toward building up your excitement to what you've experienced with the vibrator.

Another suggestion that's often helpful for some women is to increase bodily tension by breathing hard and tensing the buttocks and the legs. Contracting the vaginal muscle and bearing down is another exercise that primes you for an orgasm.

EXERCISE: THE VAGINAL MUSCLE—USE IT OR LOSE IT

Like all muscles in your body, if you don't use your vaginal muscle, it becomes weak and flabby. Many women don't even know about the existence of this muscle. Its technical name is long and cumbersome—the pubococcygeus muscle—but it's easy to identify. Put your finger into your vagina and imagine you're holding back your urine, and you're likely to feel the muscle contracting. You can contract this muscle voluntarily, as you will do in this exercise, but it also contracts involuntarily during intercourse.

You can practice strengthening this muscle by sitting on the toilet, holding back your urine, releasing it, holding it back again, releasing it, until you feel you can relax and contract the muscle at will. Make sure you're not using your stomach muscle.

Practice contracting your vaginal muscle when you have some moments of leisure, watching TV, waiting for a bus, or standing on line at the supermarket. Later you can use it in trying to have an orgasm. Flexing and relaxing the muscle won't produce an orgasm, but it will increase your awareness of the genital area of your body and increase the muscle tension that you may need to release an orgasm. You might try to fantasize while learning this exercise, a fantasy that helps to make an association between the contractions and lovemaking.

LEARNING MUSCULAR CONTROL

It's best not to overdo this exercise at first or you may end up with an aching muscle. You might start out with ten contractions, twice a day, and then increase this to ten contractions, six times a day. Each contraction only lasts a second, so the total time spent will never exceed a minute. Or you can gradually increase the number of contractions to twenty or thirty, several times a day. You should have good control of the vaginal muscle in about six to eight weeks if you follow this regime. Repeating the regime every six months or so is a good idea. In addition to the buildup of sexual tension, a fringe benefit is strengthening your bladder control.

A series of contractions right before you insert your partner's penis helps in some cases to trigger the involuntary contractions of the muscle. After insertion continue contracting and releasing to build up even more sexual tension. Your partner will enjoy feeling this muscle contract and relax against the penis. This muscular activity has been described as a valued sexual practice in the chronicles of many ancient and primitive cultures.

IS AN ORGASM NECESSARY?

Some women have thoroughly satisfactory sex lives without ever having an orgasm. However, as sexual information becomes more available, more women are curious to know what the experience is like. Other women feel tense, "hung up," or even extremely uncomfortable if they are highly aroused and do not experience any release. Certainly, an orgasm is intensely pleasurable and affords an opportunity to express many feelings and emotions that can provide the glue that binds two people together.

THE MYTH OF THE SIMULTANEOUS ORGASM

Having an orgasm at the same time as your partner is not a goal to strive for; it requires attention to timing that can serve to distract rather than enhance lovemaking. It is far better to take turns, so that each can let go without worrying too much about the other's response occurring simultaneously.

WHAT IF I DON'T SUCCEED?

Many women fear that they may not succeed at teaching themselves to have an orgasm, so they hold themselves back from trying. Others are afraid to succeed because they think it will change their whole lives—that sex will become too important, that they'll become promiscuous, etc. Most women can teach themselves to become more responsive sexually by following the above suggestions unless their fears and anxieties are so deeply ingrained, they can't give themselves permission to be sexual or to have this kind of sexual pleasure. If you feel that this is true in your case, it would be a good idea to consult a qualified therapist.

A WOMAN'S FANTASIES

An important adjunct to direct physical stimulation is sexual fantasy. Unfortunately, here, too, most women are victims of the taboos on women's sexuality. Erotic images and reveries are among the most powerful of aphrodisiacs;

indeed, they may well be as essential to sexual arousal as direct physical stimulation. Yet, many women feel guilty about their fantasies, or even try to avoid having them, because they feel there is something wrong about them. Fortunately, this attitude is changing today; according to one study, women today are far more likely to be aroused by erotic materials and fantasies and to utilize fantasies while masturbating than women only a generation ago. If you have difficulty getting into fantasies of your own, try some erotic literature, pictures, or books about other women's fantasies. Many of the fantasies women have shared with us are strikingly similar. Yours may be similar, too, or they may bear the mark of your individuality.

Beverly told us: "My usual fantasy is of a group of faceless men; they're caressing me all over. They sort of overcome me—not really violently, but as if they won't take no for an answer. It helps to keep my attention focused on what's happening to my body."

Frances told us when she engaged in fantasy. "When I'm not getting excited as fast as I'd like to, I think of times we had intercourse before we were married and how excited I felt, or I picture us making love in some exotic place."

Barbara liked to fantasize making love to Paul Newman or Robert Redford: "It's not that I don't love my husband, but I like myself better if I think a movie star would look at me."

SHARING YOUR SEXUAL KNOWLEDGE

The previous suggestions will have allowed you to become more in touch with your sexual feelings. The next step is to share that knowledge with your partner. Your ability to show him just what you like and what turns you on is an important part of taking responsibility for your own sexuality. It is an opportunity to help him give you the kind of sexual stimulation you want without any pressure on him to read your mind.

EXERCISE: SHOWING YOUR PARTNER

This assignment has two parts; you can start with either one and then proceed to the other afterward or in a later session.

Take a bath or shower together and lie down together nude. Get into a comfortable position, affectionately close —lying beside one another in whatever positions you both find comfortable. Touch and stroke and caress yourself. Don't worry about reaching orgasm, just see how much pleasure you can get. This is an opportunity for the man to fully observe and appreciate his mate's sexuality, as well as to learn about what kind of stimulation she enjoys. Most men find watching their partner stimulate herself intensely exciting.

Now show your lover how you like to be touched. Put your hand on his hand and show him exactly where, and what pressures and rhythms you find most effective. Let your mind dwell on erotic thoughts and feelings while you immerse yourself in the physical sensations you are receiving. Don't expect this to lead to orgasm the first times you try it. But do consider it a permanent addition to your lovemaking together.

EXERCISE: VAGINAL AWARENESS

This is something you can try anytime you are having intercourse. It is a way to increase your sensitivity to the feelings in your genitals during intercourse.

Have your loved one lie on his back. When an erection occurs in the course of foreplay, take the woman-on-top position. Place yourself with your knees on a line with his nipples. If you are considerably shorter than he is, your knees can be somewhat below his nipple line. Your torso should be leaning over him at a 45-degree angle. In this position, he can reach up and caress your breasts and face, and you can caress him with your hands. In this position, you can slide down on his penis, guiding it with your hand. Instead of thrusting vigorously to try to reach an orgasm, just relax and soak in the feeling of having his penis inside you. Ask your partner to move just enough to maintain his erection. Don't aim for orgasm, but rather for a complete submersion in the feeling of having his penis inside you.

Now try exploring what it feels like to move slowly in various ways. Try rocking forward and backward, from side to side. Try tightening and loosening your vaginal muscle. Consider the penis your plaything, to use as your vagina's toy. Remember, the purpose is to learn about how you feel in this position, not to achieve any kind of sexual goal. Focus on your own sensations and temporarily suspend your concern about your partner.

After you have learned to have the penis in you in a relaxed and leisurely way, you can try adding some other sensations. Try fantasy, to see if you can sink even deeper into your sensual feelings. Try moving more actively, and pay attention to the sensations. Do you find rapid movements more exciting or do you like slow motion? Learn as much as you can about your responses. If you have an orgasm with this exercise, enjoy it. If not, try again another day. Move on to more active intercourse. Place your hand or your partner's hand on your clitoral area and stimulate it while you're having intercourse; this will provide the direct stimulation that most women need to have an orgasm. You can also use a vibrator for this purpose. The use of a vibrator is something you and your partner can discuss together as one way to intensify the stimulation you may need. It doesn't reflect on either of you as inadequate; it's just another aid to greater pleasure. Incorporate it into your love play, using it all over each other's bodies. If you still don't have an orgasm during intercourse, remember that most women don't. There's nothing abnormal about your not being able to.

Experimenting with these various approaches—and others you may discover for yourself—is an important part of taking responsibility for your own sexuality. Once you find out which ones are valuable for you, you can make them a permanent part of your sexual repertoire.

Ten

Lasting Longer

CONTROLLING EJACULATION

Although you can't will an erection, you can subject the timing of your ejaculation to considerable voluntary control. There are a number of ways you can learn to last longer in intercourse, in order to extend your own and your partner's pleasure. In this chapter we will offer some suggestions that tell you how to do this.

Attitudes about how long a man lasts have changed considerably over the years. In the Victorian era, when sex was often viewed as pleasurable only for a man, a woman had little reason to want to prolong intercourse; she might even consider it a blessing if her partner ejaculated rapidly, bringing her marital obligation to a rapid conclusion. Many men evaluated their sexual pleasure and prowess in terms not of how long they could last but of how many ejaculations they had over a period of time.

As a result of the change in sexual values, sexual pleasure is now as much the prerogative of women as of men. Consequently, the question of a man's lasting longer has acquired new significance; the length of intercourse now matters to both partners.

THE REFRACTORY GAP

There is one important difference between male and female sexuality which has relevance here. As we pointed out, virtually all men have a "refractory period" after orgasm during which they cannot be rearoused and during which stimulation to the penis may even cause discomfort. Most women, in contrast, do not have such a refractory period and can continue intercourse with pleasure even after orgasm has occurred. Therefore, if a woman reaches orgasm first, she and her mate can continue intercourse until both are satisfied. However, if the man reaches orgasm first, in all likelihood that particular act of intercourse will be concluded, even if his lover is anxious to continue.

IGNORANCE, NOT SELFISHNESS

How long a man lasts can become an issue within a sexual relationship. A woman may feel that a man who habitually ejaculates soon after the start of intercourse is being inconsiderate. One woman, married for five years to a man who usually reached orgasm in less than a minute, complained to us, "He's so selfish; all he's interested in is his own pleasure. I've put up with it for a long time, but I'm fed up now. He's got to think of me for a change."

Usually a man's tendency to reach orgasm right after—or even before—penetration results not from lack of consideration, but rather from lack of voluntary control over the ejaculatory reflex. Indeed, many men who tend to ejaculate rapidly feel upset and guilty about the fact that they may not be satisfying their partners. One man told us, "I let myself down every time I come quickly, but more important, I let her down because she isn't satisfied."

It's Not Impotence

Many men feel that such a pattern of "premature ejaculation" indicates that something is wrong with their masculinity; some consider it a form of "impotence." From a biological point of view, this is very doubtful. As Kinsey wrote in his *Sexual Behavior in the Human Male,*

> It is curious that the term "impotence" should have ever been applied to such rapid response. It would be difficult to find another situation in which an individual who was quick and intense in his responses was labeled anything but superior, and that in most instances is exactly what the rapidly ejaculating male is, however inconvenient and unfortunate his qualities may be from the standpoint of the wife in the relationship.

Experience and Premature Ejaculation

There are many theories about the cause of premature ejaculation. One theory is that such a pattern of rapid ejaculation may be the result of early experience. A man may have developed it when his early sexual experience was haunted by the possibility of discovery; intercourse in a family bedroom or the back seat of a car can make quick ejaculation seem more a virtue than a vice. Some men who had their early sexual experience with prostitutes may have been pushed by them to ejaculate as rapidly as possible.

However, we see many young men with this ejaculatory pattern whose early sexual experiences did not involve fear of discovery but took place in nearly ideal circumstances —their own apartment, or a college room where privacy was more or less assured.

Another explanation for premature ejaculation is based on psychological theory—that it is a way of the male unconsciously "holding out" on women because of hostile feelings, or fear of damage. Yet there is no evidence that men with this problem are more disturbed psychologically than men who do not have this problem. We have to conclude that the cause is uncertain. But fortunately it can be treated with considerable success by sex therapy, and many couples have also learned how to treat this condition by self-help methods.

THE POINT OF NO RETURN

The basic principle for delaying ejaculation is learning to recognize the approach of the point of no return. Although an erection cannot be controlled voluntarily, men can learn to delay ejaculation.

After you develop an erection, further stimulation normally raises you to higher and higher levels of erotic arousal until a certain peak or pitch is reached which triggers your ejaculation reflex. You can tell when the reflex has been triggered because you can feel a sense of "ejaculatory inevitability"—the point of no return. Your mate may be able to identify this point of no return by the rapid rise of the testicles in your scrotum.

Your ability to identify the point of ejaculatory inevitability before it has been reached is the key to lasting longer. Once you become aware that this point is approaching, you will be well on the way to controlling the timing of your ejaculation. Unfortunately, too many men try to postpone their orgasms by *distracting* their attention from their sexual sensations. Some try to count backward from six hundred by sevens; others recite the scores of all the World Series games since 1957. Still others will pinch themselves as a form of distraction. Such efforts at distraction are counterproductive. The result is not only to reduce their pleasure but to deflect their attention from the internal sensations that signal the approach of the point of ejaculatory inevitability.

Exercise: Identifying the Approach of the Point of No Return

The purpose of this exercise is to help you sharpen your awareness of the level of arousal which precedes and will trigger your ejaculatory reflex. It requires close cooperation between partners; indeed, the woman plays the more active role. Since much of the pleasuring in this assignment is experienced by the man, we recommend that you spend some time after—or, even better, before—pleasuring your loved one in whatever way she would like, other than intercourse.

This exercise uses a technique in which the woman squeezes the erect penis in order to reduce arousal. Start by practicing the "squeeze." Place her thumb on the bottom of your penis, which is called the frenulum, with her second and third fingers on top of the penis on either side of the coronal ridge. Agree on a signal you can give her when you sense that the point of no return is approaching. It might be to squeeze her hand, or simply to say the word "now," or "squeeze."

To do this exercise, lie on your back, close your eyes, spread your legs. Your partner sits between your legs with her feet on each side of your torso, her knees bent. If this position is uncomfortable, feel free to experiment until you find one that's right for you. What is important is that the woman have easy access to your genitals.

Place your hand on your partner's hand and guide her in stimulating your thighs, abdomen, and genitals. Relax, keep your eyes closed, and temporarily tune out your partner, concentrating entirely on the erotic sensations you are receiving. Try to avoid distractions, so that you can learn to recognize the approach of the point of no return.

If you feel ejaculation approaching, give the prearranged signal to your partner. When you give the signal, she should stop stimulating you and squeeze your penis firmly, using the finger position she has previously tried out. Don't worry that it will hurt. Although squeezing a flaccid penis can cause pain, squeezing an erect penis does not. She should continue the pressure for five to ten seconds—we tell our patients to count slowly: a thousand and one, a thousand and two, a thousand and three—or until you lose the urge to ejaculate. In most cases your erection will subside, at least in part.

Most couples will miss their timing the first few times and squeeze too late. An ejaculation under these circumstances is not a failure, but part of the learning process; you will acquire a better sense of just what level of arousal will trigger your ejaculatory reflex. If ejaculation does occur, just follow the suggestion over again at another time.

If the squeeze has been applied in time so that you don't ejaculate, your partner should wait a few seconds, let the erection subside somewhat, and then begin to stimulate your thighs, abdomen, and genitals again, as before. If you don't develop a second erection, bring the session to a conclusion and repeat the exercise later in the day or on another day. Don't get the feeling that you have to produce an erection. If another erection does occur, the woman should continue to stimulate you until you give the signal; then repeat the squeeze technique.

If you have gone through the arousal/squeeze/subside cycle three times in a session, your partner can bring you to orgasm outside the vagina on the fourth trial by continuing the stimulation past the "point of no return." There should be no attempt at intercourse at this point.

It is important for any couple to learn to identify the point just before ejaculatory inevitability. If this is a problem for you, practice this exercise conscientiously, twice a week for at least a few weeks. Your feeling of control over your ejaculation will increase.

A PARTIAL SUCCESS

Gerald and Tina came to us originally because Tina was not having orgasms. They were a young, attractive couple, obviously in love, who were eager to improve their sex life. Tina did not have an orgasm during intercourse and often felt frustrated and unsatisfied after lovemaking. They both felt that if Gerald lasted longer, Tina would probably experience orgasm. We explained to them that her problem might have no relation whatsoever to the duration of intercourse, since many women do not have orgasms during intercourse no matter how long penetration lasted. However, we encouraged them to see how things would go for them if Tina did receive longer stimulation during intercourse. Since Gerald had had a problem of premature ejaculation for many years, they both agreed he would certainly enjoy his sexual experiences more if he could gain a sense of control over his ejaculations. As he put it, "I often feel they control me."

When Gerald and Tina tried the squeeze technique they stopped after the very first squeeze. Tina was somewhat offended by the position, which, she said, almost shoved his genitals into her face. "It seems like sexuality in the raw," she said. This provided us with an opening to discuss some of Tina's reluctance both to look at and touch Gerald's genitals except in a gingerly fashion. Although she regarded herself as uninhibited, Tina felt some degree of reluctance to be "blatantly sexual."

Gerald had a problem about the position. He was used to being on top, thrusting, and playing a very active role. Lying on his back elicited fears of passivity. We explained there was nothing unmanly about it; that every man should be able to relax, lie back, and allow himself to receive pleasure some of the time. We also reminded him that the goal was to increase his ejaculatory control, certainly not something which could be considered unmanly.

When they tried the suggestion a second time, Gerald signaled too late and reached orgasm before Tina could apply the squeeze. But by their next session they had become adept at working together harmoniously and were able to repeat the erect/squeeze/subside cycle three times without an accidental ejaculation. As had been suggested, Tina brought Gerald to an ejaculation on the fourth try.

After they had had several successful experiences with this procedure, both reported that Gerald was "lasting longer." It was then suggested that they try the exercise using a lubricant, such as Vaseline. The purpose of this is to create a sensation similar to that produced by a moist vagina. After three or four successful attempts with their mate squeezing the lubricated penis, many men feel a sense of control that they did not have previously and can maintain an erection outside the vagina for ten to twenty minutes of sexual play. By this time, Gerald had gotten used to lying on his back and "receiving." "I've begun to enjoy just concentrating on my own feelings. It doesn't feel unnatural or uncomfortable any more."

Gerald was concerned, however, that he would "flunk the final"—that as soon as he inserted his penis into Tina's vagina, he would again ejaculate too rapidly. He was concerned, too, that Tina was getting bored. Tina admitted that she was. Sometimes she did not even want Gerald to stimulate her before or after the exercises. "I feel as if I'm doing a job and I'm willing to do it but it doesn't put me in the mood for his doing anything to me."

After two weeks during which they had practiced their exercises fairly regularly, Tina and Gerald were ready for the next step. These are the instructions they were given.

Tina, after you've brought Gerald to an erection any way that you both find pleasurable, with either your hand or your mouth, straddle him (with Gerald lying on his back) with your knees on a line with his nipples. Lean forward and slide down on his erect penis. As soon as you've inserted it, slide off and apply the squeeze, and then reinsert it as soon as Gerald regains his erection.

Gerald, you move just enough to maintain your erection. Focus on how it feels to have your penis inside Tina's vagina. You can signal Tina to slide off and again apply the squeeze. After she reinserts your penis, you may find yourself thrusting more and more. On the fourth cycle of withdraw and squeeze, reinsert when your erection has returned, thrust, and come. It's still a training process, so keep in mind, Tina, that eventually there'll be fewer interruptions and the longer staying power of your partner will be worth the trouble.

After they had done this successfully three or four times with Tina on top, it was suggested that they try the same exercise in the side-to-side position, and later on with the man on top.

They were reminded to keep two things in mind: Gerald

was to concentrate on his own sensations; and at some point in the encounter, either before or after, he was to stimulate Tina and bring her to orgasm if she wished it.

Tina and Gerald agreed that the nature of their love-making had changed. Gerald was able to last longer. He gained a sense of control over his ejaculation that gave him a feeling of mastery and increased self-esteem. In addition, he reported that lasting longer meant prolonging the pleasure for him and made his ejaculations more intense. Tina liked the feeling of having Gerald "inside me" for a longer period of time, but she admitted to feeling disappointed that she did not have orgasms during intercourse as a result. "It's as if something shifted between us; I always felt if Gerald got fixed up I'd explode all over the place. Inwardly, it was as if I blamed him for my not coming while we were making love." Gerald admitted he had always blamed himself too. Now he could afford, as he put it, to concentrate on her more and although they didn't want to make a *cause célèbre* out of it, they both hoped Tina would eventually have orgasms in what they still thought of as "the preferred way." Although we agreed it should not be a goal that made them feel anxious and frustrated, it was certainly something they could work on together now without feeling that either of them was to blame if it didn't work out exactly as they hoped.

Although improvement in control is often seen after practicing this routine for several weeks, it is necessary to keep working on these exercises. We recommend that one squeeze exercise be done at least every two weeks for six months and then once a month for about a year. Consider it preventive medicine.

Using Your New Awareness

The squeeze technique, which was developed by Masters and Johnson, has proven extremely successful in the treatment of premature ejaculation. But if you find it difficult to work with the squeeze, there is another method that may be more acceptable for you, or you might experiment with both. Quite simply, follow the same instructions, but instead of applying the squeeze, instruct your partner to stop stimulating you when you feel an orgasm approaching. Use the routine described above, but stop stimulation each time instead of squeezing. When the female partner is in the superior position, she slides down on the erect penis in the same way, but instead of withdrawing, the man puts his hands on her hips and stops guiding her up and down or from side to side when he feels he is about to have an orgasm.

Once you have achieved a feeling of greater control over your ejaculations and have learned to focus your attention on your own sexual feelings so that you are aware of the approach of the point of no return, there are several other things you can do as well as it approaches in order to last longer. We recommend that you and your partner experiment with all of them, to find out the patterns and combinations that are most satisfactory for you.

As you feel the point of ejaculatory inevitability approach, you can withdraw your penis and squeeze the base for a few seconds. As in the "squeeze technique" described above, this pressure reduces your ejaculatory demand and allows erotic stimulation to continue without immediately triggering an orgasm.

Another way to postpone the onset of ejaculation is to bear down on the muscles surrounding the penis in the abdomen. These are the same muscles that you use for urination. It is physiologically impossible for a man to pass urine while in full erection, but by pushing down with these muscles as if you were trying to urinate, you can reduce your level of arousal, after which you can resume stimulation without triggering your ejaculatory reflex.

You can also use controlled muscle tension to enhance the pleasure of ejaculation when it does occur. Contraction of a particular muscle, the pubococcygeal muscle, tends to precipitate ejaculation and to put force behind it. This is the muscle that cuts off urination; you can identify it by deliberately stopping the flow of urine. (Once you have identified this muscle, you can sit in a chair and, without having an erection, raise your penis slightly with it.) When you feel the point of ejaculatory inevitability approaching, and you want to precipitate and encourage the impending orgasm, you can contract this muscle as if you were cutting off your flow of urine. Many men find they can increase their orgasmic pleasure if, at the point of no return, they can control the orgasm by going faster, with a pattern of pull-up-and-thrust, pull-up-and-thrust, until they finally reach orgasm.

The most important thing to remember in using any of these techniques is to continue focusing your attention on your own sexual sensations, instead of distracting yourself from them. Only by concentrating on your sensations can you become increasingly aware of the sensations just before orgasm. When you have learned this, you can delay ejaculation and let go when you want to.

If these methods don't work in overcoming your problem of premature ejaculation, it may be that you are not following the suggestions carefully, or you and your partner resist doing them because the exercises make you anxious or one or both of you feels bored or resentful (this is particularly true for the woman). Or maybe you're just not making progress. We would suggest that if any of these conditions occur you consult a qualified sex therapist. The chances are that you will meet with success in overcoming this problem.

MAKING UP FOR LOST TIME

Patty and Philip, a couple in their forties, came to us concerned about Philip's premature ejaculation. He usually ejaculated while he was inserting his penis in Patty's vagina. Not surprisingly, Patty felt resentful and somewhat bitter after fifteen years of sexual frustration. She told us that in sexual relationships before marriage she had reached orgasm in intercourse much of the time, but she never had the chance to now because her husband came so rapidly. "I don't feel like anything but a repository for his sperm," she told us. Philip, in turn, felt very inadequate sexually, especially when he compared himself to her premarital lovers, but he believed that since he had always come quickly there was nothing he could do about it.

At first Patty resisted our ejaculatory-control suggestion. "Sex has never been anything but sacrificing my pleasure to his, and I'm sick of it," she said; "this exercise is just more of all the pleasure for him and all the work for me." We sympathized with her resentment, and pointed out to her that the goal of this suggestion was to help put an end to her frustration. Her husband helped a great deal, too, by lovingly indicating how much he appreciated her help, and by making love to her by hand and mouth at the start of each session.

Because Philip had so little control, the first two sessions ended in accidental ejaculations. The couple came to us quite discouraged and ready to give up. We assured them that this was to be expected, that it was part of the learning experience, and that they were bound to succeed if they kept at it. Gradually Philip developed more and more control, until finally he was able to continue intercourse as long as he —and Patty—desired.

Philip was astonished and Patty was overjoyed at this result. His pleasure in intercourse increased greatly; she began to reach orgasm more than half the time. They greatly increased their frequency of intercourse until one morning, after a long sex session the night before, Philip failed to get an erection when Patty initiated lovemaking. Terrified, they called us up on the phone immediately to find out what new demon had come to torture them. When we asked whether their frequency of intercourse had changed, they replied, "We used to have intercourse about every two weeks; now we've been doing it practically every night." We explained that any man can fail to have an erection on occasion, and that this is especially likely if he engages in more sexual activity than he is accustomed to. Far from being a sign of impotence, Philip's momentary lack of erection was the result of the full and effective sex life they had been leading. We told them they had nothing to worry about, but that they should be sure both partners really felt like sex, and that they shouldn't put pressure on each other in their desire to make up for lost time.

When we saw Philip and Patty a year later, they told us their progress had continued. They repeated the squeeze technique once a month, using her menstrual period as a reminder, and were still getting great pleasure from their improved sex life. About a year after that, however, we got a phone call from Philip, saying that his rapid ejaculatory pattern had returned, and that he felt discouraged and depressed.

Further discussion revealed that it had been a long time since they had practiced the squeeze technique and that pressure in their lives had resulted in rather infrequent intercourse. It was pointed out that rapid ejaculation often occurs when there are long intervals between sexual experiences. We encouraged them to give their sexual life a higher priority and to fit in some "homework." We hope that they have used the methods they learned to overcome the problem they had mastered once before.

Because the directions we have described may seem a bit complicated, let's review them so you can be sure you've got them right.

The man lies on his back, legs spread, eyes closed. His partner sits between his legs, with her feet on each side of his torso. She stimulates him to an erection using her hand or mouth. He lies back, focusing his attention exclusively on himself, not his partner, and on the erotic sensations he's experiencing.

When he feels an ejaculation is imminent, he signals his wife to apply the squeeze. She counts: 1001, 1002, 1003, 1004, 1005, 1006. . . . The erection subsides to some degree, and his wife again stimulates him to erection. After four times, he ejaculates.

After three or four sessions of this, the couple tries the same exercise, lubricating the penis with Vaseline. Again, the man ejaculates after the fourth erection, outside of the vagina.

Penetration can then be attempted with the woman on top and the man lying on his back still concentrating on his own sensations and learning to further identify the point right before orgasm.

The man withdraws if he feels an orgasm coming, and the squeeze is applied; the woman inserts the penis again, and continues until the sensation recurs. The man withdraws and repeats the process, and on the next insertion ejaculates inside the vagina.

Be sure to pleasure your wife either before or after each session.

Like any learning experience, this will take time and patient cooperation on the part of both of you.

Remember to keep practicing the squeeze technique once a month for six months and from time to time after that.

Eleven

Looking Toward the Future

An Ounce of Prevention

"An ounce of prevention is worth a pound of cure." This chapter contains that ounce of prevention which, whatever your current age, will help you maintain your capacity to give and receive sexual pleasure throughout the rest of your years. Reading and discussing it *now* can serve as preventive medicine to help keep your erotic potential alive and well your whole life through.

Talking It Over

Have you and your mate ever talked about what will happen to your physical relationship as you grow older? Most couples find this subject difficult to discuss, filled with fears and anxieties that are painful to share. This chapter will give you the facts you need to evaluate those concerns. And it will give you a realistic—and perhaps encouraging—account of what you may expect.

We suggest that you sit down and discuss this chapter together point by point. Tell each other how you feel about the ideas and facts presented. No matter what your age at present, having such a discussion now will not only relieve many of your fears, but will also make it far easier for you to communicate about these matters when they are close at hand.

KNOW THE FACTS

The most important fact about your sexuality as you grow older is that you will remain a sexual being with sexual needs and sexual capacities well into your later years. This has been established by research surveys and clinical studies. As Masters and Johnson stated on the basis of their laboratory research, "There is no time limit drawn by the advancing years to female sexuality," and for men there is "a capacity for sexual performance that frequently may extend beyond the 80-year level."

In 1969, the Duke University Study on Aging and Human Development revealed that 47 percent of the couples they studied between the ages of sixty and seventy-one were having intercourse regularly. In a group aged seventy-eight and over, 15 percent were still active. Over a five-year period, 16 percent of their elderly subjects said there had been no decrease in their sexual activity, while 14 percent said it had increased.

IT'S NOT A BLANK PAGE

These facts directly contradict one of the most widespread and destructive sexual myths: that somewhere around the age of fifty, people lose their desire and capacity for sex.

A large proportion of men expect their sexual activity to

decrease suddenly as they grow older. Specifically, they anticipate having difficulty in obtaining an erection, and often they deal with their anxiety by telling jokes.

"Do you suppose old age is creeping up on me?" the gray-haired golfer asked his partner. "Lately my sex drive has turned into a putt."

"Shakespeare has been upstaged. There are no longer seven stages of a man's life; there are now three: triweekly, try weekly, and try weakly."

A patient recovering from a heart attack asked his physician if he could resume sexual activity. "Yes," answered his physician, "but only with your wife. I don't want you to get too excited."

These jokes often serve as a self-fulfilling prophecy and convince many men and women that sex is only for the young and beautiful. When people express sexual interest in the later years, they often have a feeling of guilt and shame. Rather than honoring the enduring aspect of human sexuality, it is snickered at and criticized by old and young alike.

We remember a couple in their late fifties who came to us because they had not had intercourse in nearly five years. They had had an active and enjoyable sex life in their younger years, but had mistakenly assumed that their sexual abilities would vanish as they grew older. Mal had been in the hospital with a serious illness when he was fifty-two, just about the time Kitty was entering menopause. It was a distressing time for her, and although she sympathized with her husband's illness, she also resented the fact that he was not available to give her the emotional support she needed so desperately.

The first time Mal approached Kitty sexually after his return from the hospital, she was feeling physically un-

comfortable and told him somewhat curtly to "cut it out."
The next evening, feeling quite unhappy about having rejected his advances, she took the lead in initiating sex. Mal
was ill at ease from the night before, and not completely
recovered from his long illness, but he expected that his
penis should immediately rise to the occasion as soon as an
opportunity for intercourse presented itself. Instead, he
only had a partial erection. At that point he panicked and
decided that he must prove he was still a man. He immediately mounted Kitty, pushed his semierect penis into
her vagina, and began to thrust. Since Mal and Kitty had
not engaged in their usual foreplay, Kitty's vagina was dry
and she found intercourse painful. She had also noticed
Mal's slowness to erect. Kitty believed his inability to do
so was a sign of sexual decline.

Neither ever mentioned that night to the other, but each
acted on it in his or her own way. Kitty decided she didn't
want to expose Mal to further humiliation, so she stopped
making attempts to stimulate him. When their youngest
child went off to college that year, she moved into his room
and began to spend more and more nights sleeping there
alone. Since she considered her sex life over, she stopped
trying to keep herself attractive, gained weight, and started
dressing in a way that made her appear older than she
really was. Mal, on the other hand, decided he would find
out whether there was really something wrong with him, or
whether he was unable to perform only with his wife. So
while he was away on a business trip, he picked up a woman
at a party and invited her to his room. Between the fatigue
of the trip, the drinks he had consumed, and his guilt about
"cheating" on his wife, it is little wonder that when he attempted intercourse with the woman he had just met, no
erection occurred. His partner, rather than reacting sym-
pathetically, responded with outrage: "You just lured me
up here to see if you could get it up—and you can't. You're
nothing but a dirty old man." He returned from the trip
in a depression which lasted, with only occasional remis-
sions, until the couple came to us for treatment.

Reaching a mutual decision to try to do something about their sexual impasse was their first step toward changing things. In the sessions together, Mal and Kitty began to communicate with each other for the first time in years, revealing how vulnerable each felt. Mal told of his fear of failing, his humiliation that he could not satisfy Kitty, whom he loved very much. "I don't want to get her hopes up and then leave her hanging." He was able to express the pain he felt when Kitty moved out of their room. "It was as if she had left me—didn't love me any more. I felt like a rejected suitor." Kitty, in turn, described her feeling that Mal's difficulty was related to the fact that he no longer loved her. "After all, I'm not the pretty young girl he fell in love with." She was afraid that he would feel pressured if she tried to reach out to him, or that he might even push her away. "I even talked myself into believing that he had found someone else who could arouse him."

After a physical examination revealed that there were no physical problems that would affect their sexual functioning, Mal and Kitty were encouraged to continue being open with each other, to express what it was each one needed. Both agreed that more than anything else they wanted to feel close to each other. Mal asked Kitty to join him in bed, which Kitty agreed to do, admitting how lonely she had felt in a separate room. They were encouraged to stroke and touch and caress each other with no genital stimulation at all for the first week or two together. Soon Mal began to develop erections as Kitty began to manipulate his penis with her hand and her mouth, and she responded excitedly to his loving stimulation of her breasts, genitals, and the rest of her body. Within a few weeks, they were having intercourse. Best of all, Mal's depression lifted and Kitty began to lose weight and "feel alive" again. Two years later, they reported they were having intercourse about once a week and felt closer than they had for many years. "We're talking about building a new house—as if we had a whole new life ahead."

THE REAL CHANGES

Of course, there are genuine changes people go through as they grow older, which indeed affect their sexual functioning. But these are quite different from the ones recounted in popular myth. Knowledge of these changes can help keep you from being alarmed when you see them gradually occurring.

MENOPAUSE

As women approach menopause, they are likely to have many expectations, some well grounded in fact, others not. The most obvious change is the cessation of menstruation itself. This occurs, on the average, around the age of fifty. Menopause may be heralded by a series of irregular periods, or menstruation may simply stop.

The end of menstruation is also the end of fertility. As a result, some women conclude that the inability to have babies must mean the end of their sex life, too. They may feel that if they can no longer bear children, they are no longer really women and are not entitled to sex. On the basis of years of indoctrination, they may accept the view that sex is for procreation, not also for pleasure—and thereby narrow and impoverish their lives. Other women, however, find that with all fears of unwanted pregnancy removed by menopause, they actually become more interested in sex and feel more at ease about it than ever before. As one woman told us:

> I anticipated menopause with dread, and thought it would be the end of sex and practically everything else. But actually I've gotten more relaxed about sex than I ever was before, especially with no accidental pregnancies to worry about, and no birth control to bother with.

At the time of menopause, some women experience such symptoms as hot flashes, anxiety, insomnia, and depression, perhaps as a result of hormone deficiency, reinforced by the stress of their changing life situation. Most women, however, do not experience such symptoms, or they occur only in mild form. We knew one woman who stopped menstruating and came to her doctors worried because she didn't have any other symptoms! If you do have menopausal symptoms, knowing that they are nothing unusual can help you take them in stride. In any event, the chances are any discomforts you experience during menopause will be short-lived.

HORMONE REPLACEMENT

In the years following menopause, many women develop a hormone deficiency as a result of decreased production of estrogen. The vaginal wall may grow thin to the point where it becomes oversensitive, making intercourse painful. The labia may atrophy and become thin and less sexually sensitive. The clitoris may therefore become exposed and react painfully to stimulation.

Fortunately, these problems can usually be alleviated by the judicious use of estrogen vaginal cream or other treatments to correct the hormonal insufficiency. The correction of such a deficiency is important not only for sexual activity; it is essential for general health as well. For example, a reduced estrogen supply causes a woman's bones to become porous, leading to the shrunken and bent-over appearance of some older women. This condition can be prevented by prudent estrogen-replacement therapy. Any woman entering or past menopause should discuss estrogen therapy with her physician. Such therapy is particularly indicated if intercourse is uncomfortable or painful as a result of thinning of the labia and walls of the vagina. (Many people are aware of the controversy about the possible relationship of estrogen to cancer. However, most physicians prescribe estrogen for several weeks or months when indicated and believe that there are no harmful effects from short-term usage. Certainly this is a matter that should be discussed by patient and physician.)

Mary Ann and Roger, who were in their mid-sixties, had not had intercourse for eight years. When they first came to us, they complained that Roger had difficulty in maintaining an erection when he attempted intercourse. The frustration became so great that after a while they had stopped trying. After hearing several TV programs about sex and the elderly, they decided to investigate whether Roger's sexual functioning could be restored because they missed the closeness and intimacy that intercourse had given to their lives.

Physical examination revealed that Mary's vagina had become tight and that it was no longer possible for a gynecologist to perform even a routine examination. At the same time, Mary Ann had developed a spasm of the vaginal muscles which made penetration virtually impossible. Neither Mary Ann nor Roger was aware of this condition. We pointed out that Roger's difficulty in maintaining an erection had probably developed as a result of the difficulty he experienced when he attempted to penetrate Mary Ann. It was a barrier that could not be crossed. An examination showed that he had no physical problem.

We encouraged Mary Ann to stretch her vagina with her fingers, and suggested that Roger help her with this exercise. We also recommended plastic vaginal dilators as an aid in stretching the vagina. (Your gynecologist can be helpful in explaining how to use these dilators.) In addition, we prescribed an estrogen hormone cream to restore the lining of the vagina from its atrophic state.

Within a few weeks, Mary Ann's vagina had returned to the premenopausal state and Roger was experiencing full erections. Within two months they were having intercourse again.

THE EMPTY NEST

The forties and fifties form what is sometimes called the empty-nest period for many women. The children have left home, leaving husband and wife alone with each other for the first time in many years. Believing that her function in life is finished, a woman may begin to wonder how she will fulfill herself during her remaining decades. Many women now answer this question by starting new careers. Some develop different interests or devote themselves to activities for which they could find little if any time during their younger years. Many experience a renewed interest in sex, but a smaller number use their "change of life" as an excuse to withdraw from intercourse, which they viewed as an onerous duty. For most women, these years require considerable readjustment in their life patterns. As is true at every stage of development, how well a woman responds to later life will depend on her earliest experiences, her attitudes about sex, her body image, and her capacity to form close relationships.

To a Ripe Old Age

Only as women enter their sixties is their sexual responsiveness likely to grow slower and less intense. It takes women of this age longer to attain an orgasm. They may have fewer vaginal contractions with each orgasm—although the orgasms feel just as good as ever. They may desire sex somewhat less frequently than before. These changes come on only gradually, however, as part of the general slowing up and decline of all bodily functions in the later years. With reasonable health and a good sexual environment, sexual life, including intercourse and orgasm, can be maintained into the seventies and even the eighties.

The Changes in Men

Of course, men do not experience the precise equivalent of menopause, but the years forty-five to fifty-five usually bring important changes for which men need to prepare. Many men find that these years represent the plateau of their personal achievement. Others may feel disappointed or disillusioned with the way they have spent their lives. Even if they have found fame or fortune, they may wonder whether their success was worth all the sacrifices they had to make. In any case, they are at a point where there is no turning back. Like menopausal women, they may experience hot flashes, anxiety, depression, and feelings of insecurity. Whether these common male experiences have a hormonal basis has not been established.

With increasing age, there is also a gradual slowing of

all physical responses, including sexual responses. It usually takes a man longer to achieve an erection—perhaps seven or eight minutes instead of two or three. This delay is not necessarily a liability, so long as you or your mate does not misinterpret your slower response as *inability* to reach erection. An older man also requires more direct physical stimulation of his penis, more stroking and touching, than before. The fact that you no longer get an erection simply by looking at your partner does not mean you've lost interest in her; it just means that you now need direct tactile stimulation from her as well.

An Unnecessary Misunderstanding

Another important change in men's sexuality is the lessening of the urge to ejaculate. Many couples find their sex life greatly improved by the fact that the man can last longer without ejaculating. Some couples, however, fail to understand that an older man has less need to ejaculate every time he has intercourse.

Leo and Fran, a couple in their mid-sixties, came to us because they thought Leo had become impotent. He had in fact no erectile difficulties until Fran became upset because he did not ejaculate every time they had intercourse. She tried to "give" him an ejaculation every time, as she had become accustomed to doing over the years. The result was to make sex into something unnecessarily demanding for him, and he developed erectile problems as the result of the pressure to perform. We asked Leo in Fran's presence, "Do you enjoy intercourse when you don't ejaculate?" He answered yes. "Do you feel you are missing something if you don't ejaculate every time?" He answered no. Once Fran understood Leo's feelings, they were well on their way to a restored sex life. They now have intercourse about twice a week, and Leo usually ejaculates about every other time.

Every couple should discuss the less frequent need and diminished drive to ejaculate in order to avoid the kind of unnecessary misunderstanding that plagued Fran and Leo. Nor is all the pressure likely to come from the woman; we have seen many men who felt no physical urge to ejaculate with every act of intercourse, but who thought it was unnatural or unfair to their partners not to do so. Only frank discussion with your mate can help clear up this kind of misunderstanding.*

The Changing Couple

These individual changes inevitably lead to changes for the couple. While there are children in the home, many couples relate to each other essentially as parents. After the last child leaves, they may tend to withdraw from each other. In such a situation, getting close physically, renewing the sexual side of your relationship, can play an important role in recovering the intimacy you may have lost. There is a greater need to pay attention to what your partner is thinking and feeling. You may also need to expand your areas of common interest, now that the busy world of child rearing is no longer there to share. Both should sympathize with and make allowances for the difficulties that each is experiencing at a time of change when there is a tendency to reflect on life's meaning.

This is the time to come to terms with what you want for the future, and to develop the courage to express your feel-

---

* In some aging men, the semen may pass into the bladder instead of out the tip of the penis. It later passes out with the urine. Such "retrograde ejaculation" does no harm and you should not worry about it.

ings and desires. In fact, we have found that many older people look upon this period as one of liberation—a time to renounce the old taboos and restrictions and explore what they ultimately seek in life. This may be the best way to combat the discontent and depression that may otherwise develop.

PLANNING FOR RETIREMENT

Another stressful period in many relationships comes with retirement. Often couples see voluntary retirement as an opportunity to travel, enjoy themselves, and explore possibilities that have previously been closed to them. Compulsory retirement can be much more of a strain. The woman may complain, "He's always in the house getting in the way while I try to do the housework"; the man may feel that he has been officially declared old and useless.

The key to a good retirement is to plan ahead, treating this freedom as an opportunity to expand your life into new spheres. It is essential that you develop interests outside your relationship, while strengthening that relationship itself. To maintain and even improve your sex life together can be an important way of adjusting to growing older—one you certainly should not overlook.

"USE OR LOSE"

One of the well-worn myths of human sexuality is the belief that "excessive" sexual activity in youth will wear you out so that you will lose your sexual capacities even earlier than if you had been more restrained. Nothing could be further from the truth. Indeed, many studies show that those who are more active sexually in their younger years are more likely to be sexually active in old age.

Virtually every leading authority agrees that the best way to preserve your sexuality is to use it. There is nothing that can contribute so much to having a regular sex life in the future as maintaining a regular sex life in the present. In this respect, sexual capacity is similar to muscular capacity: using it is the way to keep it.

Maintaining Your Sexual Functioning

One of the most common interruptions in a continuing sex life is ill health. Of course, during the acute phase of many illnesses, it is impossible to continue sex or any other physical activity. But restoring a normal sex life should be considered an important part of the recovery process. Sex uses little energy—no more than walking a couple of blocks or climbing two flights of stairs. And indeed, the tension resulting from sexual frustration may place you under more stress than relaxed, enjoyable physical intimacy.

What is most important in recuperation is not to avoid sex, but to avoid the stress that comes from anxiety and the pressure to perform. If you can engage in lovemaking in a slow, relaxed, leisurely way, with no hurry and no worry about failure, no need to prove anything, but just for its own pleasure, it will contribute not only to your enjoyment but to your future good health.

This is particularly important in heart disease. Men are often warned to take it easy sexually after a heart attack. As a result, they may avoid sex for months. In most cases, they would be better off resuming gentle and relaxed sexual activities much sooner—just as moderate exercise after a heart attack is healthful, not harmful.

You should take seriously the need to restore your sexual relationship after any serious illness. Ask your doctor to be specific about what you need to avoid; "no intercourse for the first week" will be far more useful to you than "take it easy" or "be moderate about sex." Try to continue stroking, caressing, and fondling when you feel like it right through the illness, and certainly during convalescence. As the sick partner feels better, you may want to include mutual genital stimulation. With such an approach, your sexual capacities should be in good working order by the time you feel ready to resume intercourse.

Of course, there are chronic physical diseases which interfere with sexual functioning over the long run. Diabetes, for example, as we have stated, leads to impotency in about half of all men who suffer from it; at present, this condition cannot be medically reversed. Under such circumstances, it is even more important that couples learn to enjoy the broad panorama of sex, to keep their physical affection and pleasure intact. We have worked with many couples handicapped by one disease or another, such as polio, stroke and other neurological conditions, who felt that they achieved a new level of freedom and understanding of their partners sexually, even though intercourse was not possible. Their sensuality deepened their communication. As one man put it, "Of course, it would be wonderful to have intercourse again, but now it's as if my whole body is much more eroticized and every touch excites me."

THE ROLE OF MASTURBATION

Masturbation attains a special importance in the later years, just as it did in the period before marriage. At both stages of life intercourse is likely to be unavailable at least some of the time. In the older years, masturbation is valuable to keep your sexuality alive while your partner is in poor health, desires sex less frequently than you do, or is otherwise unavailable. Masturbation provides relief from sexual tension, affirms one's sexual capacity, and affords an opportunity to fantasize and give oneself pleasure.

ILLNESS AND SEXUALITY

Sometimes after an illness or operation, lovemaking is avoided because of feelings of shame about bodily change or mutilation. This was the case of a woman aged fifty who had a mastectomy for cancer of the breast. For one year following the operation she and her husband had no sexual encounters, not even touching. She felt that he would be repelled if she exposed her body with the absent breast. He feared she would feel humiliated if he approached her sexually. When the couple had the courage to express to each other their fears and doubts, they were amazed how they had misread each other's minds. They were grateful that each expressed to the other that he or she wanted to be close, to touch, to love and to resume intercourse, which is what they proceeded to do after the lapse of one year.

We recommend that couples resume intercourse as soon as possible after a mastectomy. Perhaps in the future, when the custom might be more acceptable, intercourse while the patient is still in the hospital may be a means of reaffirming life and love—and overcoming the pattern of avoidance experienced by the couple described above.

A NEW BEGINNING

All too frequently the sex life of an older person is interrupted by the death of a partner or—increasingly in recent years—by a divorce or separation. Some who find themselves alone after many years of marriage tend to isolate themselves from others and feel depressed and lonely. Others throw themselves into frantic pursuit of a new partner. Most people emerge from a period of mourning and gradually resume interest in sex, hoping to find companionship and someone to love and be loved by. Becoming involved in a new sexual relationship often involves anxiety and the fear of failure. Sometimes making love to a new partner seems disloyal and unacceptable. This often results in avoidance of pleasure or difficulty in experiencing it. Talking this out with your partner or a friend, counselor, or therapist often helps to overcome the reluctance to move on to a new love.

If a long period has elapsed without a sexual partner, both men and women may be more apt to have anxiety about their performance with someone new. A dry vagina as described above may often be a problem if a woman hasn't had sex for a long time. A visit to a gynecologist is essential for a woman planning to embark on a new sexual relationship. For the man, it is important to keep in mind that the demand he is making on himself is probably greater than his partner's demand, and that even a young couple needs a period of adjustment before they can function with maximum pleasure.

THE RIGHT TO REMAIN A SEXUAL HUMAN BEING

For too long our society has regarded older people as ready for the social scrap heap—sexually as well as in other ways. We know of middle-aged people who are actually outraged by the fact that their parents are still interested in sex in their sixties and seventies. The "dirty old man" or the "sex-hungry crone" are stock images of sexual impropriety in our culture. Such stigmas are part of the myth that older people are unproductive and therefore obsolescent. Restoring to the elderly their right to be sexual human beings is an important part of redressing this wrong. And it is one which will benefit not only those who are aging today but all of us as we move inexorably through the life cycle.

Being a sexual person does not have to mean being involved in overt sexual activity. It means retaining a view of oneself as a sexual human being, in the way one feels about oneself and in the way one relates to others. This interest can be maintained by talking, reading, looking. This in itself may be satisfying for some older people; for others it may pave the way for a sexual relationship if that is desired and the opportunity becomes available.

But most importantly, everyone should recognize that the need to touch and be touched never fades. Both old and young have to gratify that need.

Twelve

Continuing Education

Pretest and Retest

If you took the sexual IQ test at the beginning of the book, we suggest that you retake it to determine whether your answers have changed now that you have had an opportunity to reexamine some of your attitudes and to expose yourself to some new and pleasurable experiences. Hopefully, what you have learned has helped to strengthen the bond between you and your partner and has contributed to a greater feeling of intimacy and closeness.

As the end of our sexual enrichment program approaches, many couples raise questions about how to sustain the gains they have made. So too the reader may feel that once this book has been put aside, old patterns will reemerge, interest will dwindle, and other activities will reduce the time and energy available for sensual and sexual pleasure.

Indeed, there is usually some degree of backsliding because less attention is paid to working on some of the principles involved, once the therapists are no longer on the scene. Many couples return for some reinforcement of what they have learned and for strengthening of their motivation to improve their relationship.

As a first step in this continuing education, we review some of the basic tenets of our philosophy. No knowledge is fully integrated the first time we are exposed to it. We need to reflect upon it, digest it, work it through in our minds, and put it to the test. We suggest that you read this review from time to time, both by yourself and with your partner, and see to what degree some of our sensual and sexual philosophy has been integrated into your own philosophy.

Sex Is Something to Enjoy, Not to Perform

The best lovemaking occurs when you can let go and allow yourself to be saturated in pleasure for its own sake. Even after years of a good sex life, many people find themselves opening up to levels of enjoyment they had not experienced before. Indeed, one of the advantages of sex within a lasting relationship is that it can make possible a kind of intimate knowledge and trust that lets you leave all striving behind.

Few things can contribute as much to the continuing enrichment of your sex life as the cultivation of your ability to enjoy yourself without having to achieve anything. If you find yourself becoming preoccupied with sex as a test or performance, we suggest that you try again some of the suggestions for unpressured, nondemand activity, such as the one for mutual touching (Chapter 3), and the erect-and-subside exercise (Chapter 8). The pressure to perform creates anxiety, one of the arch enemies of pleasure. Only when you have freed yourself from this pressure can you begin to enjoy sexual pleasure.

You Are Responsible for Your Own Sexuality

You cannot wait for someone else to come along to awaken your sexual potential. The Sleeping Beauty of fairy-tale fame was asleep for a long, long time. Nor can you blame someone else for your lack of enjoyment. Each person is responsible for his or her own sexuality. That means learning what you like and need, and finding a way of communicating these desires to your partner. Responsibility also means recognizing your *partner's* responsibility for his or her sexual responses and not blaming yourself if your partner is not always satisfied. What you can do in such a case is support your partner's efforts to find enjoyment.

Give Intimacy a High Priority in Your Life

As the pressures of daily life increase for most people, the moments of tenderness and intimacy that we need to nourish our spirits seem to diminish in frequency. Making love is often reduced to a mechanical act, boring because of its repetitive nature, a chore rather than a joyful exchange of giving and receiving pleasure. The way to prevent such a condition is to plan for relaxed and uninterrupted privacy, with the shared understanding that such intimacy need not always end in intercourse. Making a date ahead of time may be the only way to guarantee these encounters.

Of course, this does not mean that you always have to make sexual activity your top priority. Your level of sexual interest is bound to change from time to time. There will always be peaks and valleys, ebb and flow. External events, physical illness, fatigue, moods, and the status of your relationship at a particular time will markedly affect your sexual interest and activity.

What If I'm Not Interested in Sex?

Many people today are complaining that they have little interest in sex. "It doesn't mean much to me—I'd rather read a book or watch TV," and that is exactly what they do to avoid sexual involvement. Or they'll say, "We're not sexually compatible—he (or she) wants it more often than I do." Perhaps one partner will say, "I'm satisfied with only occasional sex. I enjoy it when I have it, but I don't want to have it very often. My interest and energy go into other things."

If this attitude is acceptable to you and your partner, there is no reason for you to change or feel inadequate. People differ greatly in their interest in sex and the frequency with which they have intercourse. There is no reason to feel obligated to meet standards which may not be yours.

If, however, your lack of interest lowers your self-esteem or becomes a problem between you and your partner, the first step is to acknowledge that there is a problem and then try to discover what might be causing the problem. Perhaps you are chronically fatigued or depressed or drained by the pressures and demands of a stressful life. When sexual interest is at a low level or is absent, and you want to bring about some change, the reasons need to be explored, often with an experienced counselor, so that making love doesn't seem like a chore.

CONTINUING EDUCATION

The enhancement of sexual pleasure is a process of continuing education. It cannot be learned in a crash course. As we have discussed earlier, the basic education for a trusting and caring relationship is learned in infancy, and the learning process continues throughout life and is enriched by the constant acquisition of new knowledge about ourselves and others, the experiences we have, the values we develop. It involves our total being, our personality, and our philosophy.

EXPANDING YOUR HORIZONS

Consider this book an introductory course. Continue to explore your own sensuality and sexuality, adding your own variations to the exercises and suggestions we have made.

Examine your willingness to speak for yourself and to allow and help your partner to speak for him- or herself. Communication is the only way we know to avoid or overcome the misunderstandings and resentments that are bound to arise when people are expected to read each other's minds. You may want to go over the rules for self-representation in Chapter 3 from time to time, especially if you find your relationship running into "communication breakdown."

Be sure to keep alive your pleasure in touching, kissing, caressing, and other kinds of sensual contact. Take plenty of opportunities just to hug each other, to hold hands, cuddle or sit close to each other, and to get pleasure from contact through the normal course of the day. From time to time, set aside a session just to explore the pleasures of touching and being touched (as in the exercise in Chapter 3) without aiming for sexual arousal and without proceeding to intercourse. Women consistently report that touching and being close are as important to them as orgasm. Men need to develop greater pleasure in these activities.

Try sensual pleasures that aren't explicitly sexual: looking at each other nude, swimming together, exchanging loving glances. People become estranged from their bodies in our society; we need to use them for physical pleasure in other ways besides sex.

EXPERIMENT WITH NEW EXPERIENCES

If you've always made love in one position, try another. The male-superior position is often referred to as the missionary position, because, the story goes, natives who observed missionaries making love in this way reacted to it as strange and unique to people outside their culture. A very prevalent position throughout history for people all over the world has been the rear-entry position. Yet in our culture many women object to this position. "I feel degraded," they may say, or "It's as if I'm being used." As women feel a greater sense of equality with men, perhaps this feeling will abate and this position will not be regarded as degrading. It should, instead, be simply another option to select from time to time, to provide a feeling of variety and excitement.

What is valuable in the variety of positions for having intercourse is the different psychological roles these positions allow you to play and the liveliness they introduce into your love play. For example, in the female-superior position, a man can be on his back and enjoy being catered to, stroked, and caressed. As one man put it, "Once I really accepted the idea that it was okay to lie back and enjoy, that

I didn't always have to be in the driver's seat to feel like a man, I began to really dig having my wife on top some of the time. I could see her breasts moving as she moved and that really excited me." This is a particularly good position for the man who ejaculates quickly, as he has more control than when he's on top. It's also a good position when a man is convalescing from a heart attack or other debilitating illness. Some older men, however, report greater difficulty in maintaining an erection in this position.

For the woman, the superior position gives a greater sense of active involvement. Rather than feeling "pinned down" or "as if I'm being crushed," as some women report when the man is on top, they feel free to experiment with different movements that please them. They can move up and down on the erect penis, or from side to side or with a rotary motion. They can lean forward or back, look at their partners more closely, or close their eyes and fantasize. Many women enjoy having their partners stimulate their clitoral area while they are in this position, or they can reach down and stimulate themselves, or use a vibrator. This is a particularly good position for the woman who has difficulty in achieving an orgasm during intercourse because she can regulate her rhythm, her movements, the depth of penetration for her maximum stimulation. For some women being in control may stir up fears of being too aggressive and of being rejected as a result. Learning to understand one's inner self as well as one's physical needs is an important step toward sexual enhancement.

The lateral, or side-to-side, position is another one that allows for greater control of ejaculation. It's a restful position that does not demand too much active involvement of either partner, so that it can often mean relaxed, prolonged intercourse. Its chief disadvantage is that it requires some practice to master the positioning involved.

The male-superior position is one many couples feel most comfortable with, perhaps because it best fits their mental image of how they should make love, or because it best fits the sex-role stereotype of the active male and the passive female. It also allows contact of most of the body areas of both partners, which is very arousing. It permits variety in terms of the leg positions of both the male and female, which can in itself be a source of enjoyment and a spur to further experimentation. Raising the woman's buttocks with a pillow can contribute greater enjoyment for some women. This is a particularly useful technique when impregnation is desired. Best of all, it permits looking at each other closely throughout the encounter.

There are a variety of other positions which some people may enjoy trying just to experience a range of possibilities. One of the two partners may demur at so much experimentation, feeling it's a demand on him or her, but may be willing to compromise at trying some variation on their usual position. Most people eventually settle on one or two positions they most enjoy. It's good to alternate, experimenting some of the time and then returning to the comfortable feeling of a familiar position.

VARIATIONS ON THE THEME

"It's perverse," "it's sick," "it's dirty" are all expressions used to describe oral-genital and anal sex. Because of such attitudes, many couples have conflicts over these practices.

Not very long ago, oral-genital contact as a means of sexual arousal was an almost unmentionable subject. Yet in 1958 Kinsey reported that almost three quarters of the people he interviewed admitted to oral stimulation of the penis. Morton Hunt's study in 1974 showed an even higher incidence and an increase in the number of females who were aroused by oral stimulation. From our clinical experience, although there has been a marked increase in the number of women who have enjoyed oral stimulation of their genitals, their pleasure in it is sometimes reduced by the negative feeling they have about their genitals. Women often report that they cannot relax during oral stimulation because they worry about having an odor their partner will find offensive. Trust and good communication are the key to handling this kind of situation. Don't be afraid to be frank about how you really feel, and be willing to accept your partner's reassurances. Bathing together beforehand often helps reduce concern about cleanliness and odors.

Some women do not like to perform oral sex, but may enjoy it anyway because of the pleasure it gives their loved one. There is no reason a woman should feel compelled to engage in oral sex if the act disturbs her. But she should examine those feelings of discomfort to see whether they have any real basis. A large number of women report willingness to take the penis into their mouths, and even enjoy this activity, but refuse it because the idea of swallowing semen is unacceptable to them. If this is discussed together, most men are able to withdraw in time to avoid depositing semen orally.

Some men are reluctant to perform oral sex on their partner, but enjoy the same activity when it is performed on them. Although a man should not be required to perform oral sex on his partner any more than she should be required to perform it on him, it could be of value to explore why the male partner feels this way. Perhaps such discussion may reveal the source of the man's discomfort, and lead to a better understanding and, perhaps, greater willingness to experiment.

TOWARD A SEXUALLY ENRICHED SOCIETY

A good sex life requires a supportive context, a social environment that does not undermine this most meaningful experience. Unfortunately, there are many aspects of our society that make it difficult for people to experience a full enjoyment of sex. Sexual enrichment is thus not only a question for an individual or a couple; it is also a question for our whole society. Ultimately, sexual enrichment means creating a society which encourages, honors, and supports the sexual lives of all its members. We believe there are several kinds of change—some of them already well under way—which would be particularly valuable in creating a climate in which healthy sexuality can thrive.

The Reduction of Stress

Daily life in our society involves a high level of stress which often results from the pressure to perform in a highly competitive structure. Some stress that we experience is due to the insecurity—economic and personal—that most of us face. Some of it comes from rapid social changes over which we have little control. It is aggravated by our highly mobile way of life, in which many families never settle long in one place and so much of our time is spent living among strangers.

The effects of high-stress living can be traced in the numerous stress-related diseases—ulcers, heart disease, alcoholism, depression, and many others—to which members of our society are prone. When your reactions to stress take the form of anger, anxiety, depression, or fatigue, you are probably responding in a natural way to an unnatural situation. It is also entirely normal—and almost inevitable—for such stressful conditions to disrupt your sexual and marital life as well.

Reducing the amount of stress in our lives is essential for the sexual enrichment of our society. We need a more relaxed, less driven way of life, one which provides more security and more control over our social environment. Such conditions would go far toward reducing sexual difficulties and expanding the possibilities for sexual enrichment. Until major social changes occur, however, you need to find your own ways to reduce stress in your personal and work environment.

The Deemphasizing of Achievement

As we have seen throughout this book, the block to sexual enjoyment often grows out of the belief that sex must be a "performance up to standard," that it is like a sport in which you have to prove your mettle. This attitude pervades our entire competitive society. In the world of work, we admire the "tough competitor" who demonstrates his superiority. Even in our recreation, we retain this attitude—we place a high value on sports and games whose goal is to beat the other players, and emphasize the high scorer more than the graceful player or the one who works well on a team. At the same time, we tend to place little value on activities which are performed entirely for their own sake, when no goal is to be reached, no point to be won, and no opponent to be defeated. Such activities are generally considered "diversions" from the "real business of life."

We believe this attitude needs to be reversed if sex is to receive its proper place in our society. We must learn that all the creative expressions of the self are to be valued. We should come to cherish relationships between people which, instead of being competitive, involve mutual support and encouragement of each other's self-expression. The time has come to recognize the importance of those pleasures which, like sex, prove nothing, achieve nothing, but fill us with a sense of joy, tenderness, and well-being.

The Equality of Women

One of the most important advances in the sexual enrichment of our society is the ongoing change in the status of women. Until recently, women's sexuality was widely considered unimportant or even nonexistent. Women's chief role in society was to serve and please men. They were not expected to take the initiative in seeking what they wanted, either in sex or in the rest of life.

Sexual relationships paid a high price for the subordination of women. With women forbidden to express themselves, sexual communication suffered severe blockages, leading to all kinds of misunderstandings and resentments. Because responsibility was improperly distributed, inappropriate blame of self and partner was often the result. Downgrading women's sexuality meant less sexual pleasure for women. But since there is nothing as stimulating as an excited and involved partner, this deprivation meant less sexual pleasure for men, too.

No doubt the transition to an equal position for women—and for their sexuality—will cause some conflicts and misunderstandings. But eventually the new freedom women are winning for themselves will contribute to the sexual enrichment of society. Only when our society truly recognizes women and men as completely equal and free to express themselves will we approach our capacity for sexual enrichment.

The Value We Place on Sexuality

Traditionally, our society has been generally hostile to sexual pleasure. It was equated with sin, and seen as a threat to individual, family, and social life. Fortunately this attitude has begun to change in a number of ways.

When the family was an economic unit, almost like a small business with many members sharing a wide variety of productive tasks, sex was seen in large part as a potentially disruptive force within the family—something to be controlled and limited to preserve family harmony. Today, however, the function of the family has become something quite different. The family's main responsibility is to provide for the emotional sustenance and satisfaction of its members. The enjoyment of the family relationships themselves has become a major goal. In such a context, the physical relationship between marital partners acquires a whole new importance. It comes to be valued for itself, and is seen as one of the most important supports of the family, and not a potential threat.

Finally, it is more widely accepted that sex has other functions besides procreation. Most religious groups now agree that the physical aspect of a relationship provides individual fulfillment and serves to enrich marital bonds and human relationships. Throughout our society, the equation of sex with sin is being replaced by a recognition of the importance of physical intimacy as a source of pleasure and of meaningful interpersonal involvement.

Permission to be more sexual is a major sociological change in today's world. Unfortunately, some have interpreted this new freedom as license to be promiscuous and are treating sex as a new indoor sport. Others, and they appear to be in the majority, see the new freedom to be sexual as a relief from the myths and misconceptions of the past, relief from the shame and the guilt, the barriers to intimacy that existed in the past. If you count yourself among the latter group, the new attitude toward sex gives you a second chance to acquire new information, to free yourself from past inhibitions and to honor your sexuality as a source of pleasure and a way of expressing love.

Despite these changes, negative attitudes toward physical relationships remain a powerful force in our society. Most people still grow up with the feeling that sex is somehow dirty and improper. Few have learned to feel completely good about exploring and expressing their sexuality. Sexuality is particularly off limits for the young and the old. Our society can blatantly exploit sex for commercial purposes, but it has yet to fully honor it as an important and enriching part of life at every age.

Opening up your sexual horizons does not mean adopting the philosophy of anything goes. It means selecting those experiences that are meaningful for you. Some may excite and stimulate you, others bore you, while still others may repel you. It is up to you and your partner to select from the broad spectrum of possibilities what is enjoyable and enhancing for you, and what serves to bring you closer together.

Toward an Appreciation of the Natural

Traditionally, our society has tended to view nature as an enemy to be conquered if possible, and in any case to be kept under control. Things which were merely natural were held in scorn as inferior to the products of human will and thought. This attitude was applied to aspects of human nature as well, particularly our sexual nature. The superior human being was someone who could conquer his instincts and sublimate a good deal of his sexual energy. Rigorous control was considered necessary to make sure that all physical expression remained confined and limited.

Today, our society's attitudes toward nature are changing rapidly. We no longer view nature as an enemy to be conquered. That which is natural is being accorded a new respect, as something which is precious in its own right. This approach has been summed up by the concept of the "ecological perspective," which emphasizes the value of the world of nature and urges humanity to take its place as a partner within nature rather than an antagonist seeking to conquer and dominate it.

This change of perspective also entails a new attitude toward the natural side of human life. Such human biological capacities as sexuality are being reevaluated, with their natural quality viewed as something to be respected rather than despised. The principles of sexual enrichment we have presented in this book are firmly grounded in this approach to sex as a natural and therefore valuable part of life.

Postscript: When Sexual Enrichment Is Not Enough

This book cannot help a marriage that is in serious trouble or a sexual problem that is causing considerable pain and distress to one or both partners. For example, we feel that premature ejaculation can be modified by self-help methods if both partners are motivated to work on some of the exercises suggested. If, however, the problem is severe or a source of extreme tension, or one or both of you is overly skeptical or unwilling to work on the prescribed exercises, the chances are self-help won't produce much change. Such situations require professional treatment. It is our conviction that sex therapy involves treating the marital relationship, because what is happening in bed has an effect on what is happening out of bed. Conversely, the marital interaction with all its peaks and valleys, its frustrations and joys, its boredom and its excitement has an ever present effect on making love. We recommend, therefore, that if a sexual problem is causing you distress, you should seek help together. Even if the problem existed long before you met, if one partner has a problem you both have a problem, and you are *both* involved in either perpetuating it, making it worse, or trying to solve it.

How to Find a Professional Sex Therapist

If you feel that it would be of value to you to talk with a professional about some of the questions you have regarding your sexual experience, or if you have a sexual problem that you feel needs professional help, it's a good idea to discuss this with your partner. Be open and honest about your reasons for seeking help. Try not to be critical of your partner's role in the problem, but don't assume all the responsibility for the problem either. State how you feel and encourage your partner to express how he or she feels. Seeking help is not an easy decision, but it will be another way of getting close if you decide to go together.

How do you find a qualified therapist?

You can write to the American Association of Sex Educators, Counselors and Therapists for the names of certified sex therapists in your area. They publish a directory which costs $3.00 and is updated annually. Their address is: 5010 Wisconsin Ave., N.W., Washington, D.C. 20016.

The American Association of Marriage and Family Counselors will also help you in locating someone in your area. Their address is: 225 Yale Avenue, Claremont, CA 91711. You can also contact the Eastern Association of Sex Therapists, Department of Psychiatry, Medical University of South Carolina, 80 Barre Street, Charleston, S.C. 29401.

Another good source of information for referral to a qualified therapist is your local family service agency or county medical society. You can also speak directly to your family physician, who can often direct you to the proper person, if he himself is unable to help.

Suggested Readings

GENERAL READING ABOUT SEXUAL ENRICHMENT

Barbach, Lonnie, *For Yourself—The Fulfillment of Female Sexuality*, New York: Doubleday, 1975.

Boston Women's Health Book Collective, *Our Bodies, Ourselves*, rev. 2nd ed., New York: Simon and Schuster, 1976.

Butler, Robert N. and Myrna I. Lewis, *Sex After Sixty: A Guide for Men and Women for Their Later Years*, New York: Harper & Row, 1976.

Comfort, Alex, *The Joy of Sex*, New York: Crown, 1972.

Friday, Nancy, *My Secret Garden: Women's Sexual Fantasies*, new ed., New York: Trident, 1973.

Heiman, Julia, *Becoming Orgasmic: A Sexual Growth Program for Women*, Englewood Cliffs, N.J.: Prentice-Hall, 1976.

Hite, Shere, *The Hite Report*, New York: Macmillan, 1976.

Kaplan, Helen Singer, *The Illustrated Manual of Sex Therapy*, New York: Quadrangle, 1975.

McCary, James L., *Sexual Myths and Fallacies*, New York: Schocken, 1973, paper.

Masters, William H., *The Pleasure Bond: A New Look at Sexuality and Commitment*, Boston: Little, Brown, 1975.

Offit, Avodah K., *The Sexual Self*, Philadelphia: J. B. Lippincott, 1977.

Zilbergeld, Bernie and John Ullman, *Male Sexuality: A Guide to Sexual Fulfillment*, Boston: Little, Brown, 1978.

Source Material for This Book

Erikson, Erik, *Childhood and Society,* rev. ed., New York: Norton, 1964.

Ford, Clellan S. and Frank A. Beach, *Patterns of Sexual Behavior,* New York: Harper & Row, 1970 (paper).

Hunt, Morton, *Sexual Behavior in the Seventies,* New York: Playboy, 1974.

Kaplan, Helen Singer, *The New Sex Therapy, Active Treatment of Sexual Dysfunctions,* New York: Brunner-Mazel, 1974.

Kinsey, Alfred C., et al., *Sexual Behavior in the Human Female,* Philadelphia: W. B. Saunders, 1953.

———, *Sexual Behavior in the Human Male,* Philadelphia: W. B. Saunders, 1948.

Masters, William H. and Virginia E. Johnson, *Human Sexual Inadequacy,* Boston: Little, Brown, 1970.

———, *Human Sexual Response,* Boston: Little, Brown, 1966.

Palmore, Erdman, ed., *Normal Aging I: Reports from the Duke Longitudinal Study, 1955–1969,* Durham, N.C.: Duke University Press, 1970.

Index